Nepal's Republic and India

Corridors of Power

Attention Authors

'We Convert Fighters into Writers'. That has been the motto of Manas Publications, since more than four decades. Our message to the world is that India can win the battle, not only by the bullet but also by the pen. There is no dearth of intellectuals in our country, but their knowledge is confined to them only. No sincere effort has been made by any other publisher to channelise their knowledge in national interest. That is why the talent of a large number of intellectuals, remains latent. An author transforms his knowledge, into a manuscript, and it is our job to spread his/her knowledge by converting it into a beautiful book.

For over four decades, Manas has been motivating the intellectuals by publishing their manuscripts and would like to publish your manuscript too. If you or your colleagues have any manuscript, ready for publication or are working on it, kindly contact us with detailed synopsis and the list of contents. We would transform your work, into a valuable publication. If you wish, we can also suggest you, the suitable subjects for writing books, related to your area of expertise. Manas is known for its publishing quality and commitments. We take utmost care in production and give wide publicity to the book, as well as its author, through our national and international distribution network.

Nepal's Republic and India

Corridors of Power

Dhruva Joshy
Nepal

Manas Publications
(We Convert Fighters into Writers)
New Delhi-110002 (INDIA)

MANAS PUBLICATIONS
(We convert Fighters into Writers)
(Publishers, Distributors, Importers & Exporters)
4402/5-A, Ansari Road (Opp. HDFC Bank)
Darya Ganj, New Delhi-110 002 (India)
Off. 23260783, 23265523, Res. 23842660
Fax: 011-23272766
E-mail: manaspublications@gmail.com
manaspublications@yahoo.com
Website: www.manaspublications.in

ISBN 978-81-7049-512-3
₹ 795/-

Designed at
Innovative Processors

Printed in India at
R. K. Print Services, Delhi and
Published by Mrs Suman Lata for
Manas Publications, 4402/5-A, Ansari Road, (Opp. HDFC Bank),
Darya Ganj, New Delhi-110 002 (INDIA)

Dedicated to my grandchildren

Aavani

Medhavi

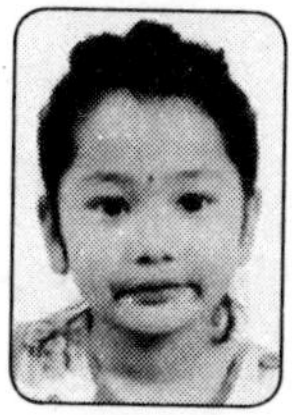

Vidushi

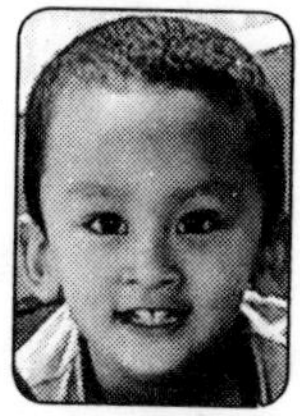

Aayan

Who give me great pleasure

with their pristine love that I treasure;

and to my wife

Veena

for holding us all together

Contents

Forenote

A Thought After Scanning the Volume

The higher a monkey rises on a tree, the more it exposes itself, was General Stilwell's dictum that holds well in the case of Nepal's politics where many a simian stands now bare and naked as never before. Unfortunately, that tribe seems to be growing faster than we imagine. This is what one feels reading the volume by Dhruva Joshy, an agro-professional.

A penchant for taking up issues of public concern, for the ancient Greeks, was what distinguished the genuine citizens from the *idiotes* (idiots) who concentrated entirely on the private affairs to the neglect of the public realm. One problem with Nepali politics is that the politicians here keep out the professionals, who in turn, rarely, if ever, come out of their professional cocoons to join politics or speak truth to power. This is what helps to maintain the culture of silence, of false consent, and of complacency, perpetuating the rulership of those who now rule the roost.

Joshy's volume breaks that silence. Unless the professionals join the mainstream politics, there will be no way out of the current conundrum and unless enlightened citizens take up the quill and the cudgel, there will be no respite from our political predicament. In this book, one can hear the voice of a professional speaking to power, his arguments rolling out with a sharpness scarcely noticed among his peer professionals and with a pungency that does not fail to leave a certain taste on the readers' mind, now bitter, now sweet, to expose the sins of omission and commission of those who have hijacked the whole process of agenda building, and hold the people their hostage, keeping the state as their captive.

At the bull's eye here is a whole range of issues – from the king's takeover to his nemesis, the Maoists. Nor does the scribe spare other parties who probably deservingly get the punch more than their hoped for share of praise. Together, the write-ups reveal not just the mind of a professional that cares about what should and should not happen to this land, but also a soul ready to share his views with the public at large, openly and unstinted. In that sense, if one ultimately becomes what one reads, the author of the volume has written in the capacity of what, in all likelihood, he truly is.

Anand Aditya

Political Analyst

Preface

Having succeeded in convincing the rabid rebels on the revolutionary front to join mainstream politics, Nepal earned its laurel in the international political arena as a nation that can resolve differences among political parties through consensus. A message that resounded across the world but now looks like a fleeting comfort. For some time past, something strange is happening to the politics of this Himalayan kingdom. As one of the most peaceful nations in the world, Nepal has now become a potential playground for revolutionary and procrastinationary politics. There are certain pitfalls that need to be watched in this political transition. The cruelest burlesque is that of the political parties and leaders whose egos larger than their combined vote base, have turned the solutions into problems, leaving everyone asking: How long can remain the country a hostage in the name of consensus?

Conventional wisdom suggests that our political leaders squandered the opportunity and thereby the drawn out transition festered in consuming irresolution pushing the nation into stasis. This book tries to analyze Nepal's tortuous odyssey that she went through after the restoration of democracy through a collection of articles delving into contemporary issues.

We have, no doubt, dethroned monarchy through an alliance of political parties. But we now face the Hobson's choice. For these political parties consensus is a flag of convenience and an existential tool incognito for their survival, which they are using as a bargaining chip to fulfill their partisan politics that is widening the political polarization.

Not responding to the mandate given by people in the CA II election, the political leaders with their brazen insensitivity are holding their peace instead. There is a chilling estrangement between the people and these leaders as these political elites are frozen in the language and style of the past but not tired of parroting a rhetorical New Nepal. Most of the leaders of the Federal Republic Front (FRF) are suffering from withdrawal symptoms as CA II election has cut them down to their size. Their flippant stance has resulted in political slowbleed for the country, where they are like schadenfreude no respect for the promises they made in the manifestos of the CA II election.

The Madhes based political parties, instead of promoting social and cultural harmony among the Madhesis and the Pahadis, are interested in the process of Balkanization to keep their vote bank intact. When talking about Madhes these leaders always evade telling the whole truth. The hegemony and exploitive policy of Pahadi ruling elites can certainly not shirk their share of the blame for the present predicament of Madhes, but this is only a half truth. Madhesi protagonists need to do soul searching sincerely. The citizens of Madhes is aware of this fact and they are, therefore, not interested if the Terai is carved as one or two or three provinces or the hill and the Terai remain together. Their cardinal issue is the socio-cultural and economic backwardness which they want to get rid of. Madhesi leaders hardly dwell on this fundamental issue. There is old chestnut about Madhesi leaders, which eloquently depicts their mind set: in power they become Nepali but once they are out of power they are Madhesi.

The story of the radical Left is no less interesting. Throughout their political indoctrination they are brain-washed and made to believe that the sole source of power is bullet. But when the Indian Prime Minister Narendra Modi was sermoning on Shaastra and Shastra (bullet versus ballot) in the Constitution Assembly, the body language of the Maoist leaders, we saw in TV, was syncretistic. The demagogue Prachand was wriggling his body, while doctrinaire Bhattarai was sniggering over, yet both were tapping the table monotonously, while the CA hall was exploding with thumping sound. We observe a very quick makeover of the radical left in the process of mainstreaming. Maoists who once spurned creature comforts to achieve their ideological goal, now to live a comfortable life and are hankering to become rich. In a very short period of time they have come out of their illusion and perhaps know that man can not live by revolution alone, when it fails to deliver.

This book is the manifestation of my personal views on the contemporary issues and the underlying processes that are at the centre of the transition, is a story of an evolution where political parties are grappling to find their role in the governance of the new republic. But the way they are wrangling ignoring the feelings of common people, reminds me of a tweet tagged in the Wikileaks: *It is okay to be idiot, but it is not okay to be found out.* And there is also a popular rhetoric in Hindi as people know everything. Let us wait and see how the people will respond when the time comes.

The names that matter in making this book are three: D.B. Gurung, Anand Aditya and Puran Bist each for their disparate reasons - for motivating me to write, publish, discovering "dark horse"in me and for rendering what was written readable. How much it is now readable or worth reading should be left to the ultimate judge of the process – the readers – to judge.

I am neither a writer nor a journalist. I am a conscientious observer and try to communicate, what I observe, without cosmetics. And the result is at your hand now. Needless to say any shortcoming one encounters with the book has nothing to do with anybody but me alone.

Acknowledgement

I am deeply indebted to several key individuals and institutions without whose support and encouragement this book would not have been possible.

Political analysis of such nature on contemporary and developmental issues is necessarily a work of individual responsibility and only the author is responsible for the interpretations of nation's political life that has been influenced by contemporary issues. But the experiences I gained while engaging for more than thirty-seven years in public sector (although in technical domain) where I had countless discussions, debates and interactions with colleagues, friends, seniors, planners, decision makers, politicians and ministers have inevitably shaped my vision to look at the nation's contemporary goings. *Nepal-China-India: The Corridors of Power* in that sense is a collective product where the social processes over the years were trying to make judgment of Nepal's political and economic crises.

I am profoundly grateful to our politicians who are – good, bad, radical, conservative, peevish, bold, unscrupulous, honest, and what not, as the beholders looked them from their perspectives – the central characters of my writings and the book would not have been comprehensive without their multihued disposition. Above all, I am beholden to my fellow countrymen, every time they have been let down by the politicians, whose voices, frustration and courage emanating from helplessness I carry in my heart, and have so imperfectly tried to put in the pages as a token of solidarity and admiration.

D.B. Gurung is not only our bold and most read English language writer, he is also a compassionately helpful friend – who encouraged me to write, read my manuscript patiently and enlightened me with his feedback. Thanks for your support.

When I was not quite certain myself of my political observations, my friend Suresh Verma took me to the writer of the then very popular column in the *Kantipur* daily, *Mohi magne dhungro lukaune*, Krishna Murari Bhandari, who introduced me with *The Kathmandu Post* (TKP). Yuvraj Ghimire the then editor gave me space with my debut article in TKP and thus starts my journey as a political observer. Later, Prateek came as the editor, he along with his editorial colleague Puran Bista continued to support me not only providing space but with a minimum cut and paste to my articles when that was deeply polarized moment in TKP. Prateek also deserves special thanks for giving his opinion on the cover of the book. I sincerely owe my gratitude to all of them. Similarly, thanks are also due to the *Repùblica* and *Telegraphnepal.com* who always provided me space in their publications.

I am indebted to Shalikram Shrestha, Professor of English in Tribhuvan University for painstakingly going through the manuscript and sharing his valuable suggestions regarding the content of the book and style of writing. Thanks are also due to my colleagues, Kiran Shrestha and Min Raj Maharjan who always responded to my short noticed calls patiently without any lassitude and had helped me performing several rounds of typing retyping and photocopying the manuscript as and when I needed them.

I owe a very special debt to my friend Dr. Arun Kumar

Singh. Believing in me he introduced my work to Manas Publications, New Delhi, India who provided all support in bringing this book out. If it was not for my friend Singh, this book would not have seen the light of day.

My gratitude to members of my family, my wife Veena, my son Viplave and my daughter-in-law Rashmi, my daughter Nritya and my son-in-law Dr. Jitendra and my friends whose love sustained me in good and difficult times and in moments of doubt. That is why I have dedicated this book to them.

Introduction

If the book we are reading doesn't shake us awake like a blow to the scull, why bother reading it in the first place?... A book must be the axe for the frozen sea within us...

– Franz Kafka, letter of January 27, 1904

I met Mr. Dhruva Joshy at an evening bash organized by The *Kathmandu Post* sometime a decade-or-so ago. It was our first personal encounter, although we knew each other through our works. We both were regular freelance contributors to the *Post*. Our friendship flourished ever since, and our meetings frequented.

It's indeed a real difficult undertaking to write an introduction to a friend's book. In the mean time, to be honest, Mr. Joshy's writings and his style have always fascinated me. When I was proposed for an introductory note by him, I was torn between two conflicting tendencies initially: resistance and temptation. Finally, I opted to fall for the latter.

A renowned agricultural scientist, Mr. Joshy tried his hand in writing (for the general mass) right after his retirement. And then followed a massive precipitation of his pent-up thoughts, blatant angers (against those who have been bunglingly sheriffing the nation) and not the less about his own nationalistic sentiments. His prose invades the reader's mind; and there undergoes an unconscious submissive assimilation, which soon persuades us that we've always possessed it but couldn't express; he invents your own mind to see things the other way round. He is a very penetrating influence, perhaps not unlike an April wind.

As are his powers as political analyst and developmental strategist. What's more important to be perceived is the radical humanity of his vision, his insistence on the bearing of moral, ethical and intellectual quality on the tenor of political and social affairs. Here he inspects the pathology of the political leadership and national affairs curiously, eagerly, with sensitiveness and intensity of passion, and without partisanship or facile ironies. He casts quite a remorseless light on the proverbial interplay between politics and the developmental drama, being intrinsically ingrained with the proclivity for satire; and these are the hallmarks of excellence in Mr. Joshy's works. Whenever something assails his mind it comes straight from his shoulder, and reels off to 'call a spade a spade,' making no bones about the consequences.

In one sentence: He's made a mark in his intellectual endeavors, period.

Yes – let's not expect a delicacy of inventiveness in Mr. Joshy's work, but a heartful feast of the country's harsh realities in conspicuous display that every Nepal's well-wisher and Nepali would love to enjoy. I've no hesitation whatsoever in stating that his achievement is unmistakable.

We can expect two major themes revolving around the book. However, most of the articles are premised on political issues, and only a few are centered on developmental theme. I for one (perhaps Mr. Joshy, too) do not have a huge appetite for 'politics'. However, as it seems impossible to lay off the public sphere (in whichever the way), in which you are a part of the same parcel. Perhaps, Aristotle was right to assert that 'man is by nature a political animal,' and to corroborate the essence of this paradox further, I quote Aung San, the father of Nobel Peace Prize recipient Aung San Suu Kyi, who maintained that 'You may not think about politics, but politics thinks about you.' Mr. Joshy, a highly educated and conscious compatriot cannot be an exception in this case, nor can he be a mere onlooker to see his country being systematically ruined and spiritually devastated by the ruling thugs. Out of these ashes, he rises and determines for a daring and decisive struggle against the tyranny of the day. His only weapon: Pen.

The selection of articles in this book painfully recalls some of the significant segments of our history spanning 2002 through 2013. 'The past is a country from which we have emigrated,' writes Salman Rushdie, 'that its loss is the part of our common humanity.' The pasts are our lost presents, the only wealth we are enriched with now; and from those valuable remnants of our past, we have meaningful lessons to learn for the present. I fervently hope that some of the articles in this collection can act as sign posts for the future of Nepal, and now it's time for all Nepalis to coalesce around a shared vision for a resilient and prosperous Nepal.

Bad politics hung thick in the Nepalese air. The new democratic dispensation in 1990 culminated into collective fiasco, despite the proliferation of media, a free market economy and interconnectivity with the outside world. Mal-administration, rotting judiciary, superabundance of strikes, insecurity, rampant corruption, apart from a total bankruptcy in political leadership – define our democratic ride of two decades and a half. Added to this, a decade long Maoist insurgency miserably pulled the country down to its knees. What's next? An unprecedented apocalypse? Welcome to a wounded Shangri-La.

So to say in a rather figurative sense, what's the smell of Kathmandu (synonymously implying the entire Nepal)? Once it had been a synthesis of a horrendously cooked meat curry, *kudeshi aachar* (pickle) that inspired an instantaneous grimace, and cheap foreign-imported war-paint. Now it's the choking fumes and bad fast food prepared by bad local cooks trained by foreign chefs! Is this progress?

Our challenges are varied at this hour. The task of cleaning the Aegean stables is not going to be an easy task. And one wonders how this fragile romance between the ruling and opposition parties ends when there is simply a deficit of confidence, rapid communication and compromise, let alone drafting a consensual constitution as mandated by the people. Where's the nation heading to?

I've deliberately chosen not to make garrulous comments about the contents of the book – let them be themselves – let the readers discover themselves what they are.

'The moment you praise a book too highly,' warns Henry Miller, 'You awaken resistance in your listener'– but I'll take my chances, although the habit of pressing books for other people is a tedious business. Still, I insist that I unconditionally admire Mr. Joshy's intellectual rigor, and it seems worth blowing the trumpets.

Mr. Joshy has triumphed in smashing the frozen sea within me.

DB Gurung

English writer and novelist

Political Commentary

1

Quo Vadis, Nepali Congress?

It was once said about the Nepali Congress (NC) that it does not need any history of its introduction as the history of democracy in Nepal is the history of the NC and it has remained always at the centre stage of the Nepali politics. Having been the most resilient political party for more than five decades, the NC has now become a political arena for unspoken upheavals – a crisis that apparently seems inevitable, *albeit* every sincere party worker, in private, looks worried and speaks against the way the crisis has been handled by the leaders. Will the NC be able to vent this crisis to a meaningful end? What will be the repercussion of these political upheavals on the NC in particular, and the Nepali politics in general? Today the NC leaders look hopeless before the public because of their oblivious state of mind to learn from history. There is a chilling estrangement between the leaders, party workers and common people, yet the leaders are frozen in the language of hyperbole.

The political fulcrum in the national politics is at a watershed in its long political history of five decades. The party of B.P. Koirala and Ganesh Man Singh known for its principles and ideology has turned into a mere crowd of mediocrity and goons. Sincere and dedicated workers are thwarted and flattery and deceit have become the hallmark of success in the party and thus the power is in the hands of irresponsible coteries. Today's NC is different. Plutocrats who have newly arisen in the politics from debauchery are deified and taken as the purpose to be in politics by the new generation. Such buccaneering leaders and workers are never questioned and punished rather always given rank and file. The impartiality of justice in the party is called into question time and again. Power and relationship have supplanted law and righteousness as the way forward. This has led to political lawlessness in the NC. A vogue of "law braking as justice" is sweeping the party and is encouraged by the senior leaders as and when it suits their purposes. The tragic event of 2050 has not disappeared from the memory of the people yet, when the so called new generation leaders vandalized the party office at Baneshwar, kicked and tore apart the picture of Girija Prasad Koirala, the then PM. This was only the symptom of a bigger problem that is looming ahead. In spite of giving serious attention to solving the problem of dissatisfaction among the party workers the leadership has always opted for a position of attrition.

What we are witnessing today in the NC is a replay of old picture show seen many times before. But the leaders are so complacent and blinded by the coteries that they are unprepared and cannot fathom the convulsions ahead. There is simply a total lack of communication between leaders. The NC is encircled with philosophy of individualism, cult of benediction and nauseous patronising attitude frustrating sincere and dedicated party workers who have always bowed to exhortation to sacrifice and worked hard for party causes and ideologies. Due to the forlorn state of mind, the entire party line is demoralised and affronted at present.

NC leaders are more political managers, intriguers and manipulators than visionary leaders with political morale who have turned themselves into a true disciple of Machiavelli. For them the political ideology and moral values are of subjective attachments only which do not bear any meaning in their personal life and behaviour. They are not tired of speaking about value-based politics, but when it comes to oneself they always act and react in a Machiavellian style putting expediency above political morality. The paradox between words and deeds of these leaders has made them look so hopeless that they are held in awe rather than revered by the common people.

The intelligentsia in the party has also turned to a bunch of mere mute and stoical bystanders on the sideline of the NC politics. Their sincere opinion and warnings had never been taken seriously by the leadership rather brushed aside and not heeded. But, unfortunately, it has taken its toll and the result is that the party is pushed into an awkward predicament of bifurcation. Adherence to certain principles and intellectual consistency always seem to be considered as vice rather than leadership quality and excellence. Downright trickery and deft political footwork have become the order of the day for NC leaders today.

The major political conflict of our times in the NC is, perhaps, due to the decline in quality of political leadership in the party. Unfortunately, most of the leaders of the present generation do not possess the intellectual instinct or personal characteristics needed to deal with the crisis of present magnitude. Their intellectual infirmity has demonstrated an inadequate sense of history and strategic understanding and they all suffer from personal ego and vested interest. The last general election of 2056 B.S. had been fought by NC projecting K. P. Bhattarai as the 'would be' Prime Minister. The NC won the election; Bhattarai became the Prime Minister only to be dethroned in a short period of time by the party itself to fulfill the ego and vested interest of powerful groups. Such is the level of ideological and moral standard of the powerful NC leaders. These leaders of Machiavellian character can go to any extent, if that will help to keep them in office, no matter what the public would think about them.

Everybody knows that the same drama was going to be replayed at the floor of the parliament by the NC to remove Deuba, its own party's Prime Minister with the support of the opposition parties (primarily, the communist groups) in the pretext of the extension of emergency in the country. The result is in front of everybody. The NC party has been thrown into chaos and it is at the threshold of division giving rise to the fluid political situation in the country.

Above all, Deuba was a favourite disciple of Girija and he is aware of all the tricks of the trade that Girija knows in the NC politics. Therefore, Deuba's reaction, to the NC's action on him, was not a surprising move. He has simply used the old tricks of Girija by pulling out the same old rabbit from the hat which Girija was rearing, at the time when he had differences with NC leaders, Ganesh Man Singh and Bhattarai. That time, if one remembers, Girija's coteries were even visiting districts in order to sense the majority in case he divides the party. Although, he could not then complete that exercise due to some reasons, today his desire has come true and he should be thankful that the main protagonist of this task is nobody but one of his most favourite disciples.

For these leaders' commitments made in public or in the party are simply an eye-wash to gain political mileage and, hence, do not bear any meaning in their lives. This is the case not only with the NC but is true with most of the political parties of the country today. To maintain themselves in power, they have all engaged in spectacular U-turns, in spite of their repeated claim that they do not crave for power and that their politics is to serve the people. Thus they simply display bankruptcy of their moral values and standard in the eyes of public. The recent statements of Girija about the Maoist insurgency is a breath-taking volte-face to gain support from communists to consolidate power in his own favour in the face of confrontation with the Prime Minister of his own party.

When political leaders try to preserve their position in power to the detriment of the ideologies and principles which they believe or the people whom they suppose to represent, the politicians can be described as corrupt. The tragedy of Nepali Politics is that political leaders have turned party principles and interest into mere bargaining counters to keep themselves in power. There is hardly any leader in the NC who believes in altruism.

If one looks at the NC's record of the past 10-12 years, it is full of misdemeanours of Girija. Be it the case of breaching the gentlemen's understanding made with Ganesh Man Singh, or removing six cabinet ministers in the name of PM's prerogative or perjury in the case of Tanakpur or the insidious action to defeat K.P. Bhattarai in the mid-term election. *Albeit*, Girija won the situation but the NC's pride has been always compromised and affronted. Recently, Girija expressed his remorse publicly and promised to overhaul the party machinery to give it a fresh look. The NC watchers are keenly watching his action. At present, he has no rival in the party to challenge him and therefore, we hope that he would show his wisdom in consolidating the party once again.

The present crisis of the NC is the upshot of lack of discernible vision on the part of the leaderships largely being dependent on the coteries, be it Bhattarai, Girija or Deuba and lack of proper evaluation of stoic dignity of the sincere and dedicated party workers. Sincere workers never queue up at the door of party leaders or Prime Minister unless they are invited and above all, they will never arrive at 4 O'clock in the morning at your place simply to pour tea into your cup. The leaders should have discouraged those who resort to such ostentations so that the party workers understand the value of hard work rather than serving as sycophants. Do Girija and Deuba have guts to kick out the coteries from their camps? If so, with all humility I request both the leaders to sit down on a table without those coteries in the larger interest of the party, democracy and the nation. For the present crisis to be resolved, the bottom-line is these leaders should leave their ego behind, when they meet each other. Let us hope that wisdom prevails at both the ends and the leaders show sagacity and vision. One likes to be surprised once in a while.

The Kathmandu Post – August 28, 2002

2

Parliament at Stake: Who is Responsible?

When Sher Bahadur Deuba, a democratically elected Prime Minister, and his break-away followers from the Nepali Congress (Democratic) party refused to prove their majority in the House to remain in power, ugly truth emerged in Nepali politics: failure to demonstrate their strategic vision in the larger interest of defending the constitution; instead they appeared more interested to hold power for a little longer time. All major political parties tried to fish in the muddy water in the name of political expediency. The recommendation of the prime minister to the King to postpone the election by a year using Article 127 brought the royal takeover. The usurpation of power by the King has transgressed the constitution as remarked by the political parties, but in the face of aberration by themselves the political parities are not unanimous in suggesting the option a constitutional monarch should look for.

Every time Nepali polity becomes fluid, these indiscernible political leaders fail to rise above the party line at the time of exigency, rather expediency always prevailed on national interest – be it the issue of Maoist insurgency, constitutional amendment, or emergency. Reluctance on the part of political leaders, who had themselves put pressure on the prime minister for postponement of the said election, on the action of the King removing the democratically elected prime minister on the pretext of incompetence in holding the election is nothing but 'hold their peace' because they are afraid of the antipathy of people, at large, against them due to their corrupt and ostentatious behavior of the past one decade. The record of these leaders are so appalling that in a short period of one decade people were of opinion that the country would be better off without them.

It is not important if the prime minister of the constitutional monarch is right or wrong in this political drama. The important fact is if the constitution has been defended by the political parties, whom the people have entrusted the guardianship of the constitution by electing them as their representatives. If Deuba's action to postpone the election is unconstitutional, as experts on constitution also agree with it, can a democratically elected prime minister, a people's representative, be removed by the king, if sovereignty lies in the people? This is a debatable issue which needs to be discussed scrupulously by all concerned parties – the people, the palace, the political parties and the legal experts – leaving their ego behind so that this hard earned democracy is not strangulated. Another side of this drama is: we all know that the prime minister was determined to hold the election in the stipulated time but leaders of six political parties conjoined to put pressure on him to postpone the election. He simply agreed to the unanimous decision of 'the all party meeting' and accordingly he recommended it to the king. But when the king on the same account removed him from the office all political parties were silent as if it was the unilateral decision of the prime minister to delay the election.

This is a deceitful act of the political parties in running the statecraft. Every conscientious person should deplore it, as it is the erosion of political ethics in the Nepali polity which is leading it nowhere. Under such circumstances these leaders cannot be exonerated from the responsibility of relegating democracy to this awkward predicament.

Of course, the major casualty of the political parties holding their peace is the 'truth'. And the truth is that democracy, once again, has been affronted. The truth is that the so-called guardians of democracy are condoning the royal action perhaps for their own survival or to gain a little political mileage forgetting that parliamentary democracy is the quintessential political device through which political, economical and social conflicts can be settled by reason, argument and persuasion and is the best safeguard against the politics of force and coercion. Common people are attracted by democracy as this system is dedicated to extending the better life, enjoyed only by the few privileged and rich people, to the general working people. Therefore, the first person to suffer from the subjugation of democracy is the common people who had fought against the totalitarian system of the past.

It is too early yet to conjecture on the future course of Nepali polity. Hindsight indicates that the fulcrum of Nepali politics has moved decisively to the Royal Palace. This process has further been encouraged by the inimical and insidious act of the political leaders towards each other when they had audience with the King in person. Nepali press is full of such accounts, although some leaders tried to clarify their stand but the common people do not take the face value of these statements or the leaders themselves. A general hopelessness of thinking pervades national life. The political parties in their lust for power are unsavoury accomplices in bringing democracy to such an awkward predicament. They are the purveyors of hopelessness, fighting to sit at the captain's chair on the Titanic for a few more hours rather than man the bridge for insuring a successful passage to democracy.

If the parliament is dissolved, does it mean that the constitution also does not function? If it is not true, who should form the present council of ministers and to whom the minister should be responsible? This million dollar question needs an attention. One of the ministers in his recent interview in a daily vernacular claimed that since he has been appointed by the king so obviously he is responsible to the king and not to the people. If it is so, how can he talk of the peoples' cause when he is not the representative of the people? I saw this minister talking on TV on the Maoist issue, and to me it looked like he himself is not convinced about what he is officially saying and not sure about what he really believes. Legally and constitutionally, if they are not the peoples' representatives, they are salary drawing ministerial bureaucrats who perform their duty as per the wishes of their mentors. An inalienable democratic right of a prime minister has not been observed in its true sense during the formation of the cabinet. These are some of the constitutional fallouts of the present political drama which need to be straightened out.

As democracy totters on the brink, we must understand that besides many other reasons, it is the failure of political leaders to live up to the events that has brought the country to this pass. We must not be tempted to believe that if democracy is shunted off, a better political system will take its place. Historical events show that if accidents happen to democracy it will not be replaced by anarchy or ungovernability. Rather it will be filled by a system of ordered totalitarian control. Whether the new totalitarian system will be of the left or the right is less important than the one that is looming. The quintessence of democracy has not found its expression in the present political drama due to which parliament has been stifled in this exercise.

The Kathmandu Post – December 5, 2002

3

Peace Talks: Apocalypse of Truth

Ever since the Maoist leaders revealed themselves in public for the high profile drama of peace talks, the Nepalese media and intelligentsia had been taken by a hysterical euphoria, conjecturing peace will prevail thereafter. How naive the Nepalese public opinion was! No doubt, it was exhilarating news to the public who were longing for peace and security, it is floundering within the present imbroglio for the past several months. People's hope of living in peace, free from intimidation and coercion is evaporating in thin air as concomitant events are unfolding the hidden truths one after another. These events are pushing the high profile drama virtually to the brink of failure.

Abduction, extortion, intimidation and human rights abuses continue. Both the government and the Maoists are violating the code of conducts, as reported by the media time and again. In the backdrop of such a scenario, even if peace is worked out between the two parties, which seems very unlikely, would the Maoist cadre, who have grown to the extent of megalomaniacs, concede to refrain from extortion? As intimidation and extortion are strengths of the rebels and termination of opponents is their political strategy, the large crowd which they show in their programmes and meetings – they often claim as spontaneous public support – therefore, is not a natural manifestation of allegiance of people for their cause. If the rebels are to believe so, it is then a talk through one's hat. On the other hand, will the security force be ready to swallow the bitter pills of restricting themselves within five-kilometre-radius and inducting the rebels in the army? What will be its connotation in terms of morale of security forces that are fighting with the rebels? Will the peace talks, under such situation, bring any tangible upshot while both the parties are sticking to their old guns? People have qualms about both the negotiating parties now, if they were tut-tuting only sans sincerity.

The Maoist crisis is one of the convoluted problems of the present Nepalese political chessboard. The Maoist escapade is an invidious exercise to continue a bowdlerized version of a dysfunctional practice which is not in vogue in the country of origin itself. Notwithstanding, it has unleashed mayhem in a country where the political crisis is inextricably bound up with a profound economic problem. Can there be a ready-made solution for the crisis of such stupendous magnitude? The Maoists, with all sincerity, know that they do not have the capability to grab the power by force, in spite of their tall talks. They are also aware that the establishment would not serve the power on a platter either. Under such an adverse situation, the Maoists are trying to gain maximum space in the political chessboard in order to become tougher on the bargaining table. Peace talks provided them with this opportunity because of the inept action and remarks of the ministers of the then government.

In the meantime, whatever reason they put forward, it has become clear to the people now that the Maoist rebels were in search of a face saving transition to come out of the jungle, as they were undergoing intense pressure from security forces, domestic as well as international public opinion. Some astute ministers of the then government, tried to manipulate the situation giving an impression that they could resolve the formidable political crisis of the country without doing proper homework and mustering enough support from the mainstream political parties. Consensus democracy was alien to them as they were not people's representatives. Many of the ministers of that government were acting in style of carte blanche and making tongue-in-cheek remarks.

That government had neither verve nor any political solution up its sleeves. The agreement of restricting the security forces within the limit of five-kilometre-radius, much to the government's chagrin, is ignored by the security force. This clearly showed the incapability of the then government to take the stock of its ramification on national security, let alone the peace talks. Under such a situation the parley was bound to go nowhere. It has proved that the peace talks hype was a damp squib and an embarrassment to the then government.

The rebels capitalized on such a state of confusion that was looming in the country to face lift their stand. If we put together the statements that the rebel leaders have spoken at different occasions after the peace talks started, they reveal their minds in their true colours. There is a wider gap between what is said and done. They may call it their strategy but for ordinary people it is a deviation from their indomitable stand. They had started the people's war to establish a republic where there is no place for monarch, but are contented with a constitutional monarchy, branded the government as unconstitutional and an extension of the old regime but gleefully sat with them on the negotiation table knowing that any agreement they reach would need to be approved by the parliament – which is non-functional at present. For common people, whom they are fighting for as they claim, it is nothing but revelation of their intention to get into the helm of power, which they could never obtain (perhaps they think so) otherwise through a democratic process, i.e., free and fair election. Equally revealing is their fear of losing the ground that they managed to gain on the negotiation table without firing a single bullet.

It seemed that the rebels, for whom power descends from the barrels of gun, have understood the power of dialogue in multiparty democracy. Therefore, in spite of all the odds, the Maoists are proclaiming in public meetings that they would not back off from the negotiation table and pressuring the government to resurrect the delayed peace talks at the earliest, lest the situation of returning to jungle reappears. They know the fact that their demands – round table conference, interim government and the constituent assembly – would not be accepted by any incumbent government unless a consensus among the political parties is met. At the same time, the rebels have yet to justify how an election for parliament and amendment of the constitution cannot meet their purpose, when they have agreed to constitutional monarchy and multiparty democracy. If they do believe in multiparty democracy then they should dare to face elections and bring about changes in the constitution as per the *vox populi*, which they claim they represent. Under such a situation if the rebels are weighing the pros and cons of entering mainstream politics, as peace loving citizens, I hope that the incendiary question "bullet vs ballot" will be put to final resolve for good. If the Maoists are good in taking the stock of the socio-economic, cultural and political ground realities of the country and the impact of globalization in every sphere of unipolar world, the leaderships would keep themselves on the negotiation table, no matter what compromises they need to go through to design and redefine their strategy.

The rebels often complain about violations of the code of conducts by the security forces, which could be true under the situation of distrust, but before whining they should put their own house in order so that people can take it seriously. If they claim that their rights are sacrosanct, they should not forget, under the same code of conduct the rights of common people and their political opponents are no less either. Therefore, a peace talk sans sincerity is dishonesty to the people. Let wisdom prevail upon both the parties.

The delay in the peace talks and the present political impasse indicates that all the players of the power game are at their wit's end. The struggle of the political parties against the regression could not muster expected public support. As the political leaders affronted public opinion by discrediting the belief of their voters with their corrupt behaviour, it is a manifestation of antipathy of the people towards such leaders. The people also rejected the Maoists because of their anti-human and anti-development actions which pushed the country 15-20 years back. The royal move of October 4 also did not receive overwhelming public support; the palace should acknowledge this bare fact. In spite of, public apathy towards the royal move of October 4, still, people have respect and honour for the crown. The king should use this opportunity and demonstrate by his deeds what he has agreed to i.e., constitutional monarchy and multiparty democracy. In order to bring the country out from the present impasse, the king, with all humility, should appeal to the Maoists to come forward to join the mainstream politics rising above their party line. After all, in a constitutional monarchy the crown does not have its own interest; the interest of the nation is regarded as the interest of the crown.

The Kathmandu Post – July 22, 2003

4

Peace, A Far Cry

No politics of a country ever likes to get into the rut. But, unfortunately, it is happening so with the politics of peace talks between the government and the Maoists. The players of the peace talks do talk about forward-looking political resolution to solve the country's formidable political crisis. Nevertheless, the politics of peace has stuck in a never-never land where the clock has stopped ticking. The facilitators look pathetic and sound like waffle. They are politicking more than facilitating the peace talk. Because of their political association their neutrality required for the job is very much in question. In the issue of boxing the security forces within the radius of five kilometres, the facilitators simply remained as on-lookers and did not brother to clarify the truth to Nepalis. A serious question was raised on the sincerity of the government in agreeing with the decisions reached in the talks because of their silence. They found it safe in rolling with the tides. Next time anyone tells me about the uprightness of these facilitators, I shall simply pooh-pooh.

The announcement by the Maoist Supremo on Wednesday agreeing to sit for the third round of peace talks is, indeed, going to be a turning point in the Nepali politics, by and large. However, this turning point would not be of the kind ordinary people are looking for. On the day, the rebel leader made his announcement public to participate in the third round of peace talks, the media reported that two soldiers were killed and three seriously wounded in an attack by the Maoists. The killing and other forms of human rights abuses are continuing unfettered in spite of the cease-fire agreed by both the parties. The weeks ahead will serve as an indicator of seriousness of the rebels, putting aside the communist rhetoric, towards resolving the inextricable crisis of the country.

It seems peace is knocking on the door, still at a distance. Also in the past, peace was at hand, yet it slipped away. Who was responsible for it? The Nepalis know who wants what now. It is beyond doubt that all are keeping their fingers crossed for the resumption of the stalled peace talks. It is also true that the people expect the government not to leave any stones unturned to make this event a success. Still, very few people believe that things will fall into place once the peace talks get on to the right track, particularly under the situation when the rebels are forwarding conditions one after another for the government.

There is an element of distrust associated with the rebels, which they make use of always, to shift blame on the government if things go against their interest. But this time, for the rebels, it will be not easier said than done as the current mindset of the government has revealed that it is prepared to go extra miles to ensure that the peace parley is not disrupted. But looking at the past track record, it is difficult to convince oneself that the rebels would not eat their words again. Let us believe that it would not happen this time.

By setting new conditions for resurrecting the stalled peace talks, the rebels have demonstrated that they are no easy pushovers. And at the same time, they have upped their conciliatory gestures conceding to the fact that they would not walk away from the peace process either. In reply to the government's request to resume the peace talks, the rebels' concerns (apart from their previous demands) – the participation of political parties in the peace process and a minimum common understanding between the King, the political parties and the Maoists to resolve the differences – have exposed some chinks in their escutcheon.

Not long ago the rebels were thundering that unless all the agreements reached in the pervious talks were implemented, the third round of peace parley would have no meaning. But expediency does a lot of wonders in politics than anywhere else. The rebels are beholding the light at the other end of the tunnel, which leads to the corridor of power. Being in the proximity to the power lane, the rebel leaders seem so desperate now that they are even compromising their stands based on which they had shown a 'dream world' for their cadres. Will it be easy for the militant cadres to sacrifice the dream for which thousands of their comrades have given their lives, gone to perdition and branded as desperadoes?

It is becoming clearer than ever that not all rebels comply with their leaders in handling this People's War. The disillusioned comrades reveal the fact that they have been promised a total revolution for bringing compete political changes. The continuation of killing and intimidation by the rebels is a manifestation of the resentment against the shoddiest political compromise their leaders have made to gain space. Under this dichotomy even if a peace accord is agreed upon, the dissatisfied faction of the rebels may continue the war in the name of total revolution they promised in order to establish the 'dream world' of proletariat. If this happens, the permanent peace, that the Nepalis are looking for would still be a far cry.

The rebel leaders know it explicitly. They are also aware of the fact that it is beyond their capability to contain these militants without giving them what they have been promised. An awkward situation is looming ahead in the country for which the Maoists cannot blame anybody else, but themselves. These leaders are, neither running away from the peace talks nor do they want to conclude it, adopting a Fabian strategy.

The Kathmandu Post – August 09, 2003

5

After Hapure Talks

Ever since the peace talks at Nepalgunj and Hapure suspended yielding nothing, but a deadlock, the turning and twisting of Rubik's cube of politics of constituent assembly versus constitution reform by the players of Nepali politics were all-time high. All of a sudden this is grounded by the announcement made by the Maoist supremo declaring that the cease-fire, the code of conduct and the peace talks have lost their relevance and do not hold now. This is not an unexpected outcome, rather, in spite of all the optimism it is an anticipated fate. To be more exact, it is a calculated political destiny of the peace talks. When Dr. Baburam Bhattarai rejected the government's roadmap for forward looking reforms brandishing it a first-aid only to a cancerous disease, it was an indication of communist psyche of self-righteousness that had prevailed upon wisdom. The common people smell a rat in the frequent veering of the Maoist stand as a ploy to get their cadres out of government custody, withdrawal of red corner notice and price tag on the heads of the rebel leaders. If it is so, the Maoists were impudent enough to play with the sentiment of the people, who were sincerely rallying for the success of the peace talks. The major casualties of the Maoists' volte-face will be our democracy and later the people at large.

A decade ago our democracy seemed set within the constitution which was so meticulously prepared by the representatives of the political parties and experts. Opinions from the common people and civil societies were invited during its preparation. It was then claimed as one of the best-written constitutions in the world. The same constitution has become a document of contention today and the democracy that has been practiced based on that document is at watershed in a very short period of time. Who is responsible for it, the constitution or the democracy? Neither, rather it is the inept political leaders who were unable to act in the true spirit of the constitution because of their debauch behaviour on one hand, and on the other hand, it is much to the chagrin of the palace to be confined as the constitutional monarch. One thing is now clear to the Nepali people and that is no system, ideology or ism is perfect, when it has to deal with humans. We have the experience of both the authoritarian (Panchayat) system and the democracy of twelve years. It was a failure on both the counts because of the exclusionary attitude of the elites of the power centres in the statecraft.

As the rebels have rejected the government's dossier on political reform, both of them have locked their horns on the issues of the constituent assembly. The common people feel that they have been robbed of their desire of living in peace partly due to the arrogant and obtrusive posture of the rebel negotiators, partly due to the government's failure to take the rebels into confidence and to a certain extent due to the incompetence of the facilitators in unfolding the knots of the bone of contention which everybody knew was sure to come up on the negotiation table. While the entire country was desperately worried about the future of the peace talks and rallying public support for its success, the facilitators seemed hoping under the influence of sheer fatalism about the upshot of the dialogue. Is it not their failure, that the facilitators were unable to push through to the rebels the general consensus of the people that seven years of bloodshed did not do much good either for Nepal or Nepalis? Perhaps the hospitality of the rebels at Hapure was so satiating that they forgot to talk their heart. Now the common people have to pay for the facilitator's holding their peace.

One of the annoying problems in the government's handling of the peace talks was the exclusion of the political parties and the people at large in the whole exercise. Most of the negotiations were undisclosed to the public in the pretext of security reasons. Nevertheless, the government could not solely be blamed for the lack of inclusiveness. It is the political parties who are giving the government a cold shoulder and trying to make hay while the sun is shining. The royal place, the political parties and the Maoists all are playing Machiavellian politics putting aside the interest of the people and the country. This is a serious situation and a set-back for the tottering Nepali democracy. The palace and the political parties are in a state of classical stand-off, a conflict that could only result, if ruthlessly fought to finish, in the victory of one side over the other. The present situation between the government and the rebels is also heading towards the same fate. If this happens, will foreign interests remain as mute on-lookers only on the side lines? What fate will the Maoist cause meet at that time; it is difficult to anticipate at present. But one thing is very clear that the country will be pushed into a political quagmire. Should we not learn a lesson from Afghanistan?

The intervention by foreign powers, the Maoists are so vitriolic about, is there because of the government's policy, the Maoists actions also seem no less responsible to provide an opportunity to proliferate it to the present magnitude. The secret hideouts of the Maoist leaders in foreign soil, their dubious contacts with illegal outfits of the foreign countries, their anti-human tactics and illegal resource mobilization from foreign countries were equally responsible for such intervention. Under such circumstances, it seems derisory when the Maoists whine about foreign intervention in our internal matter while they themselves are wallowing in external support in the name of fraternity.

The press release issued by the Maoist supremo on Wednesday has poured cold water on the hopes of the common people to live in an atmosphere of peace and tranquility. It is easy for anyone to send tough messages across the line and that is likely to be heeded also if the king's nominated government is weak and lacks self confidence and public support. If government, which is branded as non-representative of the people, opts for the constituent assembly under pressure from the rebels, what will be the legitimacy of such an agreement? The Maoists know it, yet are going for it. Is this not the double face of the Maoists? The rebels often talks of the people and for the people, if the rebels are so serious about the people, the constituent assembly that they claim for the people let it be agreed and approved by the people and not by the nominated government or the Maoists. Should this not have been thought by the vainglorious Maoists? Perhaps, it will open a new vista in the peace initiative. It is still not too late as the saying goes – 'Better late than never'. *Pro bono publico* let wisdom prevail on expediency.

The Kathmandu Post – September 6, 2003

6

Will the Bell Toll?

After the royal action of October 4, our democracy totters on the brink and so does the country's political situation veer between two authoritarian spectres of right and left. In between, the leaders of the political parties, the Five or Six Samurai, are acrobating as a tin-God taking people for a ride. What one witnesses on the drawing board of the three political forces hitherto, reveals that none of these forces seems trustworthy – neither the constitutional monarch (as the king claims), nor the political parties, and nor the Maoist rebels (who are not tired of talking about people's cause but hardly heed people's voice). These political forces do not seem either sincere or accountable to the people.

Almost everyday, public concern about the current national crisis has been highlighted through scores of meetings, interviews and the interaction programmes in the capital and other places in the country. In these events, the views expressed by the leaders of the political parties for the resolution of the crisis somersault unseemly so often that they are notoriously infamous for being consistently inconsistent.

It is baffling for the common people and is the manifestation of their self-betrayal and intellectual hollowness.

Ambiguity and deviousness have been the hallmarks of these political leaders. The concern of these political leaders to defend democracy lamentably fell short of expectations of the people today. They do talk about the present national crisis, but the word 'crisis' has lost its urgency as compared to their apparent lust and downright trickery to hold power. After the eight rounds of their so-called movement against the regression these leaders are at their wit's end, neither is it possible for them to join the King nor can they support the Maoists.

The Maoists, on the other hand, are not opening all their cards, for they know that their so-called people's war cannot be won by the bogey of terrorism and intimidation. *Albeit*, some of their demonstrated intents are noteworthy, yet the means they have been following to achieve their goal are not appreciated by the people at large. Can the Maoists be ever trusted? In the light of annulment to cease-fire, their credibility is, once again, at the lowest ebb. They are adopting a policy of blow hot and cold. Next, their unruly cadres are proving Achilles' heel in their movement and the leaders are groping how to contain them if they need to surface up as a political force. If this happens, will the Maoists be ever accountable to the people?

When the whole country is terror-ridden due to the inhuman act of the sanguinary Maoists leading to a holocaust, the palace is living in a backwater. Following the dismissal of the Deuba government, the king looking resolute, appointed Chand, and later, Thapa as the Prime Minister as a retribution to the political parties. A high drama of peace talks with the Maoists was enacted, where the rebels were successful in gaining most of the strategic benefits rendering the government as a loser on all counts except for a fragile cease-fire, which too the Maoists used for their strategic purposes.

On the question of guarding the national interest, the Chand government measurably failed by agreeing to provide citizenship to the refugees unwilling to return to Bhutan. This was an anti-constitutional and anti-people decision. The Chand government, for such ignominious decision, was taken to task overwhelmingly by the people. It also failed to bring the political parties into agreement. And thus it had to resign. The Chand government has proved a failed experiment, very much anticipated, in the account of the palace for which nobody seems ready to take accountability. Why? If the Nepali people are sovereign, should their qualms not be answered to their satisfaction?

The king, playing cool on the suggestions of agitating political parties, has appointed Thapa as the next prime minister in a hope that he would be able to resolve the present political crisis of the country. But all indications are pointing out that this experiment would also meet the same fate as the previous one in all counts.

It seems, the untold policy of the palace revolves around the contentious issue from the point of democracy. Ever since the October 4 royal action, there is a widespread belief that the palace is keen to regain its abdicated authority and seek a palace-dominated style of political system. No matter what one calls it, the political analysts look at it as an attempt to settle 'old scores' by the palace and pro-panchayat jingoes with the democratic forces, which had relegated the active monarch to a constitutional one by the revolution of the 1990. Notwithstanding this, King Gyanendra has publicly declared that the constitutional monarchy and the multiparty democracy will remain as the guiding principles of our political system.

The appointment of the prime ministers, after the disposition of the elected government, by the king himself was a political contrivance in the hope of getting popular support. But unfortunately, it did not pay any dividend either to the palace or to the nation at large. This action further distanced the political parties from the palace providing them an opportunity to apprehend the King's intention. In spite of the efforts of the foreign diplomats and other well-wishers, the king seems not in hurry to entertain the political parties in resolving the current political crisis, rather allowing a process of attrition against them. No matter what it is, the country's political crisis has deepened further pushing Nepal to the brink of a failed nation. In order to rescue the country from the current political quagmire, the royal rhetoric on the occasion of Dashain needs to be translated into deeds.

Nepalis always like to believe that the king does not make mistake and the impeccable crown remains as a respected institution. But the indulgence of the crown in the statecraft, by the unilateral interpretation of the article 127 of the constitution has dragged it into controversy. In recent days, a chink has developed in this faith. If this deepens further there is every possibility that the Maoists and anti-palace forces will use this card against the monarchy and democracy. Where it will lead to is anybody's guess.

Under the pretext of settling old scores if the democracy is shunted off, we must not be tempted to believe that a better political system will take its place. There are indications that, in all likelihood, the void created by the demise of the Nepali democracy will be filled by a totalitarian system. It is not of much importance, if the new totalitarian system will be of right or left. Does the bell toll for the political leaders?

The Kathmandu Post – October 25, 2003

7

Looking Beyond Conceit

When the second peace talks failed, the common Nepalis, at large, were taken aback and felt affronted. Once again, the desire of living in peace had been wrested from the people due to obduracy and ruse. Gruesome violence has been let loose again by the Maoists in the capital and around the country as their way forward to achieve their goal. This has shaken the faith of the peace loving people in the country and abroad equally. The nominated government is helpless and puts on a long face in front of public outcry.

The sham constitutional government failed to involve the parliamentary parties in the government. In order to hide its failure, the government was impudent enough to nominate party cadres of its favour for the local bodies, otherwise elected by the people. On the other hand, in sheer frustration of its inability to resolve the Maoist problem peacefully, it adopts the idea of a 'unified command system' – a surreptitious way of militarization. A sense of fear and mistrust has prevailed around us. Because of the deteriorated political situation in the country, a sense of hopelessness has pervaded at all levels of national life. Everything is in a fix. Revival of peace also seems unlikely at this moment making it even more illusive.

Perhaps, most depressing of all is the forlorn state of mind of the people. They are, alarmingly, becoming inured to the apathy of the government. They are beginning to get used to bombs, abduction, strikes and *band* conjoined with a general feeling of national failure. This has left Nepalis desperate and demoralized today.

In the backdrop of such drift, a message must have driven home to Maoist camps that intimidation and targeted killings of unarmed civilians, political opponents, and security forces do not pay-off to muster up public support for their political agenda of republic and constituent assembly. Had it been so, the common people would have demonstrated on the streets demanding for the constituent assembly as they have been rallying in support of the peace talks. But, on contrary, even after wasting more than 10,000 Nepali lives the Maoists are nowhere near to their goal of republic, rather, it is becoming clearer with each passing day that they have been fighting an anachronistic war which is turning pointless, transforming this Shangri-la into a killing field.

Although it is no fair to draw an analogy between the Maoists and LTTE of Sri Lanka and IRA of Northern Ireland, nevertheless, one could learn a lesson from such a protracted insurgency where nothing but peoples' lives have been wasted, country's pride is affronted and national unity and integrity are whittled away. Negotiation have paved the way for settling even inextricable political issues which military might could not for more than twenty years in those countries. Should not the rebels learn from the international experience of such nature, rather than satisfying their ego in the name of dogmatism?

At this hour of peril, none of the major players of Nepali politics are seemingly candid and discerning in resolving the crisis, let alone the demagogue Maoists. In spite of adulations the apathy of the Palace to bring back the political normalcy as of pre-October 4 royal action is eerie and weird. Why is the Palace not in synergy with political parties, the main players of the multiparty democracy, in spite of their allegiance to constitutional monarchy? It is a topic of interest to political analysts to regurgitate. Notwithstanding, the handling of the recent appointments to the constitutional positions by the Palace debunks its psyche indicating propensity to a constructive king vis-à-vis constitutional king.

The king, on more than one occasion, has declared his commitment to constitutional monarchy and multiparty democracy. Nepalis believe that his commitment is by choice and not by compulsion. But, surprisingly enough, one finds a state of incommunicado between the king and the political parties. The political parties, which represent the people, are eschewed grossly in the political decision-making process. In the absence of dialogue between the king and the poitical parties the blame for current political instability in the country after October 4 royal step seemingly lies on the Palace. For the simple reason, the charges under which the Deuba government was dismissed, inept in holding election on the stipulated time, remain valid for the nominated governments of the king which too are finding difficulty in holding the said election. This means that Deuba's suggestion to the king to extend the house was correct to avoid the current political debacle, as holding the election then was also not possible. This could possibly be taken as an entry point by the king to break the standoff and call Deuba to initiate the political dialogue. After all, nobody is a perpetual friend or foe in politics.

The message to the Palace is also loud and clear. Mere changing the guard in Singh Durbar would not deliver the goods the Nepalis are longing for – the peace and security. To solve the present political imbroglio, it demands scrupulous sagacity from the king as he has an upper hand in the political game at present. Now it is evident to the Palace also that exercising Article 127 of the constitution repeatedly neither fills in the political vacuum nor does it bring the constitution back on track. Hitherto, it has turned into a political hot potato. This is also clear now that the political parties and the bigoted Maoists, because of the international politics, are no easy pushovers. Hence, this is high time that the king should take the Nepalis into his confidence and act accordingly looking beyond ego for the sake of the country and the people.

As a political analyst if one recalls the constitution of 1990, it is acquiescence between the king and the political parties where the monarch has accepted the multiparty democracy and the political parties show allegiance to constitutional monarchy. If handling of the country's politics by the Palace after the royal action of October 4 is a harbinger of the desire of the king for the constructive or active monarchy, it annuls the above-mentioned understanding and provides a pretext to the political parties to disregard the bilateral understanding of which the constitution of 1990 is an outcome. The recent rumbles in the party lines about the republic could be viewed from this respect. Will this embolden the Maoist demand? This needs to be closely watched.

If democracy is all about good governance, accountability, keeping moral practice in politics, protecting people's right and fulfilling the social justice, etc. then our political leaders have miserably failed in all counts. They are infamous as self-serving, disloyal and immoral political personalities in the country, *albeit*, they are the representatives of the people. Our constitution has provision to deal with such wrong-doers, in whatever capacity they are, for their culpable offence and for the king the constitution has contemplated as a highly exalted institution that never does wrong – a highly venerated sentiment of Nepalis towards the institution of monarchy. This is possible only when he is a constitutional monarch and not constructive or active king.

The Kathmandu Post – December 20, 2003

8

The Rendezvous

The year 2003 has passed away into the dark lane of history. It will be remembered as the year of strife and turmoil. The year started and ended with the continued gruesome violence of the bellicose Maoists, the political imbroglio and the constitutional impasse. All aspects of national life had been overwhelmingly best ridden by these political issues. The nation witnessed the beginning of the media hyped-peace talks between the government and the Maoist rebels only to be aborted because of obduracy and intemperance on the part of the negotiating partners, and the brazen infidelity to the people on the part of the facilitators. Much to the people's chagrin, the country with great pain recorded the meaningless deaths of thousands of Nepali lives in the name of establishing an outlandish dictatorial philosophy of one party rule in an era of globalization and free market.

The year ended with a blow to the Prime Minister and his Information Minister, who was also the general secretary of the Rashtrya Prajatantra Party. The Prime Minister ran around the SAARC region on grand diplomatic tours, but he could not hide the fact that his government has lost the usefulness at home. The party asked its leader, the Prime Minister, to resign from the post as he failed to fulfill the mandate given by the King, and later it sacked the Information Minister from the post of the general secretary of the party. In response, the Information Minister has challenged the decision of the party which he has every right to do and in turn he needed to prove that the party took a biased and illegal decision. But, to the dismay of law-abiding citizens, he broke into the party office, which was an act of flippancy and rowdyism by any standard. In politics, if ends are to be achieved by violence, then discipline and democratic values are bound to wither in the party. Who cares?

The constitution is in a state of derailment. The elected leaders are being ruled by the nominated ones in the name of constitutional provision. The conservatives under the umbrella of Raj Parishad are manipulating the situation to consolidate themselves, showing unnecessary activism under the pretext of informing the ground reality of the country to the king. The political parties engaged in the fight against the regression also failed miserably to rise above their party lines on the issues of national interest and guarding democracy. Because of their in-fightings their credibility is at the nadir of people's expectations. This could be the reason for the lukewarm response from people to their clarion call for the fight against the regression.

Albeit, the student organizations of the political parties have been successful in raising the dipping mercury to its height on the street when the government arrested their leaders and announced that they would be tried for the charge of treason. The students could not be cowed down, but rather took over the street in defiance of this decision. Their protest started growing bigger by the day as the civil societies of different walks of life came forward and joined the movement. The government sans people's mandate could not bear the heat of the students' agitation and ultimately had to succumb to their demand by releasing their arrested leaders. Encouraged by this, the students are not in the mood to calm down their protest. They want to open a debate on a very far reaching issue of monarchy vis-à-vis republic. The body language of the belligerent students indicates that they can go to any length if the need arises. It is too early to speculate on how the students will take their demand further. But one thing is obvious that the students were always the torch-bearers of the formidable changes that have happened in this country, be it a social or a political one.

The major political parties like the NC and the UML eat their words, whenever they have to speak their minds on this issue. The public stand of these leaders veering between pole and post suggests that they like to keep rare this issue, as carrot and stick, in case they have to strike a hard bargain with the palace. The bare fact is that a chink has been developed in all the parties' lines on this issue. It will be interesting to watch in the coming days how the political parties resolve this issue which may reverberate throughout the country.

The New Year has dawned with some heart-warming news as well. As the saying goes, *Better late than never*, the king has resumed the process of dialogue with the leaders of the political parties. Seemingly, the ice has been broken but it has a long way to melt. One must not forget that the country faces hard questions without easy answers. When we are in negotiation, we should not subscribe to the Bolshevik hangover that everyone who disagrees with us is our enemy. Engagement and dialogue wherever possible should be the state of art in solving the problem of such nature.

In the past one year, the credibility of the palace has slid down on the scale. Rumours have wings. Some rumours fly very high in the political quarters, such as the Maoists are blue-eyed boys of the palace. There is no way common people would ever subscribe to this view. This provides an opportunity to the king to join together with the constitutional forces and isolate the Maoists and help bring the much-needed peace and security to the country. Also for this matter, the consultation must continue in spite of the pessimism expressed by some leaders after the first audience with the king.

If the initiation of the dialogue by the king with the leaders of the political parties could be taken as an indication of the paradigm shift in the palace in viewing the existing political and constitutional deadlock the country is facing today, then a common ground could be found even among the divergent views the political parties are adhering to. The bottom line is "the multiparty democracy and the constitutional monarchy." The common people are hoping that both the king and the political leaders would show sagacity and statesmanship so that the rendezvous does not turn into Hapure talks.

The Kathmandu Post – January 13, 2004

9

Political Parties and Royal Antipathy

Some issues are exigent while others are ineluctable too. The question of transferring the executive power by the King Gyanendra to the elected representatives of people is both exigent and ineluctable in democracy. In order to solve this formidable issue, the Parliament either needs to be restored or an all-party government formed and/or the election held, let alone the problem of the Maoist insurgency.

The apathy of King Gyanendra towards the first two options has left the elections as the only way out to bring back the popular government in place.

Recently, the King in Pokhara has referred, not promised, to hold the election by April next year. But who will hold the elections and when is a big concern of the major political parties.

The hand-picked government is bent on holding the election. If that happens, the political analysts conjecture that the political parties, in all likelihood, would not acquiesce to participate in such exercise. For holding a free and fair election, they have been demanding an all-party government.

To make the situation further disconcerting, the Maoists have poised to whack at any place and at any point in time, if the government embarks on the insidious apple-cart of the election. They have proved their brinkmanship in the broadsides of Bhojpur and Beni recently.

On the backdrop of this ground reality and the credibility of the nominated government to hold the election in question appears illusive and discomfiting more than ever.

Therefore, the reference to the election at Pokhara's royal address is an astute effort to project a democratic posture to the international community. Whether it works as an anodyne remains to be seen.

What has been haunting in the minds of the people is a question since the King dismissed the elected government on the ground of ineptitude to hold the elections on stipulated time. But, on the same count, the King was eerily mum when his hand-picked government was kicking its heel for one and half-year hiatus to hold the election promised by him.

What explanation the King Gyanendra could have for this delay other than the one the then prime minister Deuba recommended to him to defer the election? If this is the case, it suggests that whatever maybe the intrigue of the then prime minister Deuba, his assessment to defer the election because of the deteriorating situation does hold water.

If one goes by this analysis, the King Gyanendra, to emulate his decision of October 4 royal move, should have no hesitation to restore the Parliament unless the King has other political game plan up his sleeve than what he has publicly proclaimed on more than one occasion that his desire is to hand over the power to the elected representatives of the people.

Whether the royal take over of the executive power was right or wrong is an issue that is debatable, as there is a deluge of opinions and arguments in favour and against the decision.

Notwithstanding, if one puts the events into perspective for a dispassionate analysis of the political situation, with all fairness, one tends to believe that in order to avoid the constitutional void in the face of the then prime minister Deuba's recommendation, the royal action was a contrivance that unfortunately culminated in the political stand-off between the two constitutional forces bringing the country to an unsavoury quagmire.

The country could have been saved from the distress, if the monarch had acted as a true guardian of the 1990 Constitution and warned the Prime Minister about the upshots of political vacuum giving him a chance to behave more scrupulously than turning the table on his face. The King, taking the executive power in his hand, perhaps was buying time to see if he could push his active role in the country's governance by fanning the frustration of common people against the political leaders. The Panchayati jingoes, the Raj Parishad conclaves and the CIAA have been used to meet this end.

No doubt, these political leaders, when in power, have condescended to venal practices with impunity during twelve years of democracy. It is commendable on the part of the CIAA that these kleptomaniacs are brought to book.

Albeit, its uncanny silence has exonerated the leaders of Panchayat era, who gulled the country for thirty years non-stop, have remained scot-free hitherto. Such preferential action did not help the CIAA in any way.

The King's preference to these sham democrats to govern the country and being at odds with the political parties suggests that his action does not match his words.

The King aspires to be the constitutional monarch of the twenty-first century, but enjoys outlandish customs of royal tour of felicitation in tandem without much benefit to the nation or people at large. The King Mahendra and the King Birendra had also embarked on such exciting quest of rediscovering the country and its people. In spite of the adulation to such royal tours of felicitation, the country's plight did not change during the thirty years of Panchayat regime, rather it had slide down in the rank of least developed countries further. Surprisingly enough, nobody was held accountable for the misdemeanour but now impudently the buck has been passed onto the twelve years of miss-rule of political parties solely.

In an era of IT, there are, definitely, more efficient means available to update one without necessarily being profligate. The scribe has no intention to conclude that public felicitations are not worth, but on the other hand, the King has every right to receive public felicitation, particularly at the time when the people are putting hopes on him that he would bail the country out from the present inferno.

But the kind of felicitation extravaganza one has witnessing is not called for when the country is in mayhem due to the Maoist insurgency, political fluidity and abject poverty. When life of common people is in perdition such ostentation does not help in assuaging the sufferings of the people. It would be naïve to assume that the monarch is unaware of it.

The country, at present, is caught in a war with the Maoists, who are bent on establishing a republic. During his tour of public felicitation, people with much hope appealed to the King to restore peace in the country.

Hindsight suggests that the Maoists would not deliver anything on a platter to the King or political parties either. Peace is only possible when the King and the political parties conjoin to deal with the Maoist insurgency politically.

It is an opportunity for the monarch, often criticized for it has lost its relevance, to realize the advantage of dealing with the political parties and prove his wisdom and prudence to stop the country from being a banana state.

The bottom line is that – ego and antipathy needs to be annulled. If the crown and the political parties cannot be good friends, they can remain as intelligent rivals.

The Kathmandu Post – April 15, 2004

10

The Royal Palaver

The monarch wanted not only to be visible but audacious also. This is the royal wish flaunted by King Gyanendra in his address to the people of the Far Western Region during his recent public reception. It has seemingly debunked that the late King Mahendra is perhaps his role model. The people are, therefore, apprehensive of his move of October 4, 2002 as his desire to be heard.

Much water has flown through the Bagmati river, since then. The way-ward Maoists, although anachronistic, have made their presence felt throughout the country. For good or worse, anti-regression agitation has instilled the Republican sentiment in the Nepali psyche. Above all, the awareness level of common people, after the restoration of democracy, has upped to the extent that they cannot be subjugated further.

Little wonder that the strong avidity of the King for an active role in politics, defying the 1990 Constitution, has brought the crown head on collision with the political parties. But these parties, hitherto, have remained the supporters of the constitutional monarchy, no matter, what their frontal organizations are pushing on the streets. The King squandered eighteen months testing the mettle of these political parties, if they could be marginalized from the mainstream politics by goading the public distaste for them into a fury.

But much to his chagrin, it did not turn on the way he wanted and the crisis spiraled up further deepening the distrust between the political parties and the monarch.

But, to everyone's surprise, people are incessantly spouting on the streets in defiance of the prohibitory order of the handpicked government, showing their resentment against the October 4 royal move. This is giving a clear and loud message that the Nepalis are not in a mood to acquiesce to anything shorter than the 1990 Constitution with further guarantee that the King would not be allowed to take any anti-constitutional step and security forces remaining accountable to Parliament.

It would be naïve to assume that the King is unaware of the fact and the present political stand-off could be resolved by extricating the agitating political parties. Perhaps, the monarch under fatuous optimism believed in the process of attrition and, therefore, much fraught with his social and religious commitments to the extent he has been quoted as a Himalayan Nero by David Rohde in *The New York Times* (April 21, 2004).

The public felicitation under the shadow of Beni broadside was the zenith of insensitivity and apathy of the King towards Beni's hapless citizens.

The King has failed miserably in all counts – in aligning the constitutional forces, bringing the Maoists into the mainstream politics and creating a congenial environment to conduct a free and fair elections and thereby bringing a political stability.

Filled with the despondency, the King has opted for reconciliation with the political parties to resolve the present imbroglio. He has put forward, once again, the card of politics of audience to them. Hindsight suggests that the audience with the King without agenda, in the past, have proved nothing but a garrulous act to smoother the heat of the political agitation against the regression.

The political leaders, in the past, who had the audience with the King, had borne the burnet public diatribe for their imbecile conduct. Therefore, this time these political parties are not kicking up their heels and have demanded to create an environment prior to the consultation for a meaningful outcome. Otherwise, it will be another hackneyed approach showing royal apathy towards resolving the formidable issue.

By putting the ball of the dialogue in the royal court, the agitating political parties wanted to be sure if the royal invitation is not yet another decoy. A burnt child dreads the fire. This has left with the King a limited option to consult with the vassals sans popular base like *ex*-PMs, and leaders of the political parties, except a few, whose obsequiousness have rendered them into political buffoons. These time-servers neither win the election nor could their parties ever come into power. What sort of advice these subservient politicians would provide to the King does not require much effort to anticipate as they are a crowd and not a cynosure of crowd.

It is now evident that the King has no magic wand to solve the constitutional crisis of his own creation. The people have paid enough price for the escapade of the royal lust; if at all the dialogue is the only way out of the current impasse. In this regard, if the royal initiative is a pensive move, the King must take the leaders of the agitating party into confidence, not the titular leaders, so that the royal initiative does not turn into another palaver.

To make this consultation a meaningful exercise, the King should meet the leaders of five agitating parties in group rather than individually and refrain from his exclusive idea in the choice of the head of the government. He should agree to the demand of revival of the parliament even though it seems *non sequitur* from the point of view of the Supreme Court (SC).

No doubt, there are deluges of arguments against and in favour of this proposition. But taking cognizance of the country's plight, the SC should also rethink and revise its judgment in the interest of the people and the country, particularly if this saves the country from being a failed state. *De minimis non curat lex*. Can the SC show this courage?

The Kathmandu Post – May 8, 2004

11

New Royal Initiative

Cold facts can be denied neither by the hot statements of political leaders nor by the reticence of the King Gyanendra which is more revealing. The truth is that the country is caught between intemperate political leaders and the power hankering monarch. To make the situation further eerie, the gory act of the bellicose Maoists in the name of peoples' war has been turning as *ad nauseam*. This has left the country to choose from the good, bad and the ugly.

It would not be an exaggeration, if one says that the present predicament of the country is the result of indiscernible dissonance of political leaders and the usurpation of power by the King in the greed of being audacious in the governance of the country. In spite of his commitment, in public, to the constitutional monarchy, the King seemingly looked oblivious of the constitution snooping into selecting a candidate for prime minister.

Dispassionately, if one looks into the account of the state affairs of the period of the royal take-over, one finds little respite from misrule and chagrin. The Maoist insurgency has grown into a full-blown war with devastating consequences. The country has witnessed more bloodshed in the last three years than ever. Both the security forces and the Maoists are going berserk in their actions bringing ignominy to the country in human rights front.

People are displaced, abducted in hundreds as cattle, local representatives are dismembered, institutions are dysfunctional, chief district officers in many districts sleep in army barracks at night, and governance is frustratingly ineffective. The King Gyanendra had directly ruled the country for almost two years as the purveyor of good governance, only to fail. In these years, he experimented with appointing two prime ministers of his choice. Both of them failed in holding the said election and bringing the Maoist rebels into the mainstream of national politics. Thus, the country is pushed into the abyss of constitutional limbo.

The drama of consultation was enacted several times by King Gyanendra meeting with the leaders of the political parties and people of different walks of life. All proved a hackneyed approach because of his pent-up pathological hatred, as has been revealed in the newspapers, regarding the political leaders. In democracy it is the people, who judge the political leaders if they are good or bad, not the King.

King Gyanendra failed to provide a civil government to the country for more than three weeks keeping the country sans government. It gave an impression that the Palace is incapable of getting the country's affairs right. The country is, without a doubt, in a worse state now than it was eighteen months ago when he usurped the executive power and installed a hand-picked government. He has created this dilemma for himself.

The stark reality is that King Gyanendra has overstepped the constitution by dismissing the elected prime minister. Thus, the simple fact is when you are wrong, you are not right.

After the royal consultation with all and sundry the royal flippancy for public opinion was, as if, not enough to Nepali sensibility, came another shock when the Palace put a notice to recommend a name for the post of Prime Minister.

How could King Gyanendra, who reminds the political leaders not to drag him out of constitution, roughshod over constitution making a mockery of democracy?

This shows, on the part of the Palace, a lack of business acumen the public mood on the one hand, and on the other, it debunks the intention of the King to select the prime minister of his choice.

Because of such contradictions the country, at present, is in turmoil and its future is so uncertain that the question is not "Will democracy survive in the country?" or, "Will the monarchy continue?" It is "Will Pashupatinath save Nepal?"

Bringing back Sher Bahadur Deuba in the office of Prime Minister again obviously suggests that King Gyanendra has realized his mistake for which the country has had to pay a heavy price. The King's rule by proxy is responsible for the abasement. This is an unwanted situation, which the King could have avoided by eschewing the avid of being constructive or active monarch.

In these three years, the two constitutional forces, who are supposed to be the two sides of a coin, distrusted each other to the brinks of sidelining each other. Are the political parties only responsible for this state of the country?

When Sonia Gandhi in India declined the chair of Prime Minister, the common people here were asking the leaders of the political parties to learn a lesson from it. Apparently, I also felt the same way. But after a little while when I tried to find the analogy between the situations, I had to change my earlier popular analysis. Wondered whether the King could demonstrate the grace and dignity of Sonia Gandhi to save the country?

If the answers are affirmative, I reckon that the great democratic exercise recently practiced in our neighbourhood would provide prudence to the Palace in solving the impasse between the King and the political parties.

Deuba's induction, if it is a new appointment or reinstatement, will remain as a matter of debate for the political parties. But, it is a step forward towards bringing the derailed constitution on the track, if sovereign right has been inculcated in the people as has been said in the royal communiqué. The road ahead is bumpy. How far Deuba could convince other political parties, particularly the agitating ones, to join his all-party government is a litmus test for his success. Let us wait and watch.

The Kathmandu Post – June 4, 2004

12

Pot Calling A Kettle Black

In the aftermath of Deuba's enthronement as the Prime Minister, the Communist Party of Nepal (UML), once a redoubtable ally in the anti-regression agitation of five political parties, has seemingly lost the *savoir faire*. This party is of the view that the dissonance among the five parties of the alliance in recommending the name, in response to the royal call for the position of the Prime Minister, has baulked Nepal, the general secretary, of his prey. Much to its chagrin, it has not only wriggled out of the alliance of the five parties but thrown its support to Deuba's incumbency as well. The stooping of the UML was, as if, not enough to Nepali naiveté, came another surprise when it declared that the regression has been partially corrected.

Whether the UML's astute calculations provide the country a respite from the current political imbroglio is a matter of wait and see. Yet the sentimental pleas of the UML leaders like 'solution of regression should not be kept as prisoner of indecisiveness of four parties of alliance' etc. could not masquerade their intention. Perhaps, it would not take aeons to clear if their adroitness is an aberration or business acumen.

The UML is always blamed for its double standard and ambiguous stand – be it the issue of accepting the 1990 constitution, be it the Mahakali treaty, or joining the RPP government in the past. It seems that ambiguity and deviousness have won the day. Its statement admitting regression as partially corrected has put it in the defensive.

This is the apotheosis of ambiguity as deft political footwork in the name of practical politics. On the one hand, this has excoriated the UML while on the other hand, it has exhilarated the King as it endorsed his volition without stint.

Nepali psyche is not as oblivious as the UML is. Not long ago, Nepal and his myriad of cadre were chanting incendiary slogans on the streets to fight against regression. Today, it has deserted the alliance when the partners in the rump are still continuing the agitation on the street. The UML has not been able to justify to the Nepalis its elopement from the Ratna Park.

At this juncture the visionary leader Madan Bhandari and his ability to take decision based upon political insight and instinct for right directions conjure up in the minds of common people. This style of leadership in the UML has disappeared now and the party is bestridden by a class of political pygmies feigned as leaders. Not to name anybody, recently in an interview of a domestic TV channel, a UML leader, would be minister, when he was cornered by the TV anchor, was explaining as a high school teacher that communism does not advocate one party system, notwithstanding, the fact that his body language was not supporting his words. They simply lack the essential instinct of Bhandari that provides confidence pertinent to take decisions.

The Nepalis would not subscribe to the whining argument of the UML that because the alliance, particularly the NC, did not want to forward the name (?) to the Palace, therefore the King had made Deuba as the Prime Minister. Even the novice of politics would not believe it for a moment. As the applications of more than thirty buffoons were thrown into the dust-bin, looking at the track record of the palace, the name forwarded by the alliance would have received the same fate. Was the UML looking for that humiliation or was it a lust of chair? It simply raises a big question on the sincerity of the UML vis-à-vis anti-regression agitation.

Meanwhile, the UML has made public its conditions to join the Deuba government, but listening to the jabbering of its vainglorious intellectuals, it was almost certain from day one that the UML would join the Deuba government. So is Deuba waiting restlessly to welcome them in the government. It is not inexplicable to understand the UML obsequiousness. Perhaps, Nepal reckons what he had failed to gain by joining the alliance of the five political parties; he could get it by supporting the Deuba government. The prelude to the crow has already been played when he said, if Deuba government fails, it should be his turn to head the government next. Does the bell toll for Deuba? It is in the interest of Deuba, when he sups with the UML he must have a long spoon.

The King, while appointing Deuba as the prime minister, has explicitly given three mandates for the formation of all-party government, establish peace and security bringing the Maoist insurgents into the mainstream politics and conduct election for the parliament within one year to hand over power to the people's representatives. Arguably, the minimum common program is stretching too far in a style of red-herring between the incumbent parties to securing their respective interests in the government and forgetting the primary imperative the people are looking for – the formation of an all-party government.

If all the political parties of the dissolved parliament do not join this government, how is it different from the previous two hand-picked governments? How is the UML going to explain this? Will the UML have courage to acknowledge the pot calling the kettle black?

Interestingly, the magic wand of Article 127 is still in the hands of King Gyanendra. No matter what the UML thinks about regression, partially or entirely corrected, the King can still use the Article, if he wishes so, under his discretion. If the King deems that the mandate given to the Deuba government is not fulfilled, which is very likely to happen, will the UML have gall to join the four party alliances again on the streets? Or, will it support the Palace for a guided democracy, which it is contemplating as a potential grand design?

The Kathmandu Post – July 1, 2004

13

NC's Trojan Horse

The unfortunate incident at TIA befalling Girija Prasad Koirala has ineluctably drawn a lot of attention. The event was a routine security check, if Koirala is to be taken as an ordinary denizen, but if one looks at him as a leader of the opposition and four-time elected Prime Minister of the country, the locale would signify a different connotation. Similarly, the reactions of the common people towards this fateful event vis-à-vis Koirala in person is a kind of love-hate story. If one puts bits and pieces of the events of the past few months in perspective, a picture pops up of pathological hatred from the line of generalissimos and their commander against Koirala for his political posture, whereas, in the social front, he has been a *bête-noire* for a certain section of the society.

The unpleasant event, for whatever motive it had happened, reverberated throughout the country, since he is the leader of the country's biggest political party – the Nepali Congress (NC). If one likes it or not, this message has been clearly felt in every quarter.

I was impressed by the NC not because it is a political party that has always remained in the forefront of Nepali politics and had defeated the despotic oligarchic rule of Ranas in 1950, or it had relentlessly struggled for over three decades and finally, with its allies, succeeded to bring down the authoritarian partyless Panchayat regime of the King. For me, it was a movement of conscience and reform that was fervently committed to the democratic and liberal human values more than any other political parties of the right or left. It was warm, idealistic and vibrant and had always honed its policies against inequalities and exclusive attitude in all walks of life. Therefore, to me, it was more than a political party – a philosophy of social advancement.

But, after the restoration of democracy in the country, something strange is happening with the NC. The party which was once known as *avant-garde* of Nepali democracy has been whittled away to a party of mediocrities and kleptomaniacs. A party, once, known for its ideology, courage and candor, is now bestridden by male factors, parochial vision and pecking order. A party which was resilient in nature turned so stiff-necked that it has led to a vertical division of its own. Above all, what non-plusses me the most is that these myopic leadership, at every level, those who have relegated the party to a crowd of subservient and time-servers, are not remorseful at all for bringing the NC to such an awkward predicament.

A culture of extra-constitutional power-centre sans accountability is the order of the day, within the party rank. Democratic exercises are found only in the speeches of the leaders and not in their behavior. If we recall the ninth general convention of the party in Pokhara, it will provide insight to the party functioning. There was an agenda of constitution amendment and many good proposals were on the table, but the chair made a ruling and an official bid was passed without discussions on the other proposals put forward by the members. As the chair said 'pass' all his sycophants around him also shouted 'pass' 'pass' and the official amendment was declared accepted. This is the kind of democratic exercise one finds in the party's rank and file.

The party which has led the revolution for establishing democracy in the country for more than once is now weirdly run in an adhoc manner where system goes into abeyance. Most of the tall leaders of the party only squint at it and are uncannily lackadaisical to open their mouth. Amusingly enough, when they come to power, these wannabe do-gooders are the ones who are never tired of talking about observing a system in the bureaucracy. What a ruse! Because of the inadvertence of these leaders, the party has turned into a mere crowd of vassals devoid of principles and ideology.

An example of discomfiting adhoc culture in the party rank and file was enacted in the recent past when the party president Koirala announced, on his own, to pardon the comrades of the break away NC and opened the gates for their home coming. No doubt, it is a very plausible move to unite the divided NC and a rational decision, particularly when democracy in the country is at peril. Nonetheless, an organization is not run by words of mouth, but by its rule-book which ought to be followed in making decisions, unless you are a despotic leader like Saddam, Idi Amin or Duvalier whose words were *coup de grace.*

Another example of abhorrence for the rule-book by the party rank and file is the sacking of the elected president and general secretary of the NSU, a front-line student body of the NC, recently. As the decision of termination of the student leaders was not approved by the Central Working Committee (CWC) of the NC prior to its implementation, one NC leader had reacted that the NC leadership has a culture of acting in haste and justifies their actions at leisure. This action of the secretary general was sure to draw acrimony in the meeting of the CWC.

Party president, Koirala, in order to save his protégé from backlash, avidly undertook the onus of approving the removal of the NSU student leaders himself. To the dismay of the CWC members, next day, he unilaterally indorsed the termination without giving student leaders a chance to explain their case. It was tantamount to authoritarian behavior reflecting that the NC is run under distasteful degree of paternalism.

A backwash of such nonchalant behavior of Koirala on the elected members of the Central Working Committee of the NC denigrates them to nothing but a mere crowd of political buffoons waiting to endorse his waffle. What can one expect from such servile pygmies but thralldom? The NC, today, unfortunately seems all too often to settle for the average, the mediocre, and the corrupt. Judging by the CWC meeting held recently, it seems that the party has no intention to learn and Koirala is still entrusting the task of running the party to similar set of servitors. These were the same henchmen who used to be gratified to pour tea for Koirala at 4 o'clock in the morning, when he was in Baluwatar.

After the restoration of democracy, the NC has changed from a party of workers to a party of leaders for whom conviction of democratic culture is a matter of convenience only. Admittedly paternalism has won the day in the party. This has declined the morale of the stoic workers for whom the word Nepali Congress was synonymous with democracy. The floating generation of rootless leaders who dominate the party are more comfortable in Bangkok than in their own constituency. The decline started the day Kishunji passed the party presidency to Koirala. It has been a slow disintegration since then reaching its grand finale in the year 2002 when the NC was vertically divided. The Trojan horse did not come from Troy; it very much exists in the party itself.

Because of such contradictions there are many workers in the party, who seriously believe that the country faces an inevitable authoritarian future; the incident at the airport with Koirala is a harbinger to it.

More ominously, the NC is losing the support earned by its past glory. This is the party that withered away in power. It has failed to realize that managing power is difficult and a professional task unlike fighting against power. Power has swayed the party away from its workers and people. The word 'congress' which was the legendary hallmarks of change and modernity is now held in derision. If one happens to be in the districts the morbid state of the party's district committees reminds us that they are there to simply indorse what is being asked by the centre. They are like a jalopy which does not move but rattles only. Under such dismal situations, the thundering sound bites of the octogenarian leader hardly provide respite from despondency.

The Kathmandu Post – September 11, 2004

14

Chasing the Peace

The volte-face of the Maoists, saying that they would not talk with the servitor of the old regime but only with its master marks a critical turning point in the murky and uncertain process of the peace parley. It has torpedoed the hopes of the Nepalis who are yearning for living in peace, and without doubt, has also disappointed the peace-loving people of the world at large. Interestingly, the same belligerent Maoist leadership, who had peace talks in the past, though it failed, with the then government nominated by the King with much fanfare in the media, is now abrasive towards the similar dispensation to sit at the negotiating table. Why? Is it because the Maoists have unleashed untold misery onto the Nepalis and, therefore, dither? Or, is it a calculated strategy to put the King in an invidious position flagging that they are cognate with the Palace?

To the dismay of the Nepalis, the latest stand of the Maoists is preposterous. It seems that within the Maoist leadership a struggle between guns and rational politics has reached its zenith. The platitudinous remark of the Maoist Supremo in response to the call for peace talks has made peace more and more elusive.

In spite of assurances given by the leadership on more than one occasion, the Maoist cadres have not refrained from inflicting atrocities on common people and media persons. Rather their individual killings, abduction, extortion, intimidation and threat of attack on district headquarters have heightened, suggesting that die-hard bigots are in domination in the present leadership. These belligerent leaders seem not to believe in peaceful political negotiations and are bent on anachronistic dogmatism of Chairman Mao that power only springs from the barrel of the gun. Under the context of changed world order, the above tenet does not hold water. Therefore, the Maoists should drive a lesson home that war only happens when politics fails or is made to fail by the people of vested interests. Otherwise, there is always a peaceful solution to a problem.

But Nepali Maoists seem oblivious to the fact that Mao's country itself no more subscribes to the belief of Mao, and has recently proved that power could be transferred peacefully without the use of guns. Jiang Zemin, without shedding a drop of blood, has handed over his most powerful position of commander-in-chief of China's armed force to Hu Jintao, the incumbent Chinese President and general secretary of the Communist Party. This smooth transfer of power has been exalted as a landmark in the modern Chinese political history. Why don't the Maoists here learn a lesson from it and change themselves befitting the times that we live in today? In the last decades of the past century, the world has witnessed landmark changes in the field of political systems, where totalitarian dispensations were replaced by a pluralistic and competitive world order. In most cases, *quid pro quo* was the hallmark of conflict resolution. When the Maoists say that they are in favor of resolving the conflict, they should realize two things; first, when one is in negotiation one cannot have everything one wants, and the second being that there is always an alternative to war, provided there is such a wish.

The government, after many flip-flops, has announced peace talks finally. Prime Minister, Sher Bahadur Deuba seemingly looks cautious with his steps. His extra-civility and political savvy evince that the government is pensive and committed to resolving the political issue peacefully. The Maoist high command, instead of responding to the government call for peace talks, has retorted to asking six questions as a condition to agree with peace parleys. These queries could have been put on the table once they start negotiations. But, unfortunately, obduracy prevails and the Maoists forget to care for the wishes of the Nepalis.

Prime Minister, Deuba's task of bringing the derailed peace talks on track does not appear any easier today than when it failed earlier. Even with all good wishes, the peace talks, if it happens, would not turn a cakewalk for both the warring parties. Unless the Maoists come out of the rut and the government demonstrates more inclusiveness the much-hyped peace talks will prove nothing than waffle.

The Kathmandu Post – October 4, 2004

15

Fidelity and Dilemma

The Information and Communications Minister, Dr. Mohsin's apprehension about the possibility of an authoritarian dispensation in the future has ineluctably drawn the attention of media. Unmistakably, it has triggered off severe criticism from all sectors of the nation. As the issue gotten hot, he swiftly disowned his remarks, in front of media persons who had called on him at his residence. He said he had been misquoted by the press and reported that he had implied that the king would takeover and install an authoritarian rule. He clarified his position and explained that he was actually pointing at the danger of totalitarian rule by the Maoists, if this government failed. In either case, if Minister Mohsin's hypothetical machination comes true, whether an apple falls on the knife or the knife on an apple, the loser is the Nepali people who may have to feel the brunt of an authoritarian rule once again.

Minister Mohsin is not representing any political party in the government; however, he is an important member of the RPP. His position as the kingpin in the Cabinet is conspicuously visible as he is the nominee of the King. In spite of the CPM-UML's resentment he is also the spokesperson of the government. Thus, considering the feathers in his hat, his remarks could not be taken as fortuitous. Political observers are looking for the *raison d'être* of his recently made remarks. If Dr. Mohsin's sudden threat is taken at its face value, the verbal calisthenics he indulged in is nothing but his personal cliché-ridden opinion. On the other hand if the remarks are viewed on the backdrop of the forthcoming royal visit to India, it could be taken as the reading-of-the-minds by the king through one of his servile representatives in the cabinet. Or else, it may be a harbinger of the king's desire to jettison PM Deuba as his usefulness is waning.

While reading the statement of Minister Mohsin, one might have been taken aback. But, for those who know him, it is his fidelity to the lord rather than to the ideology and that explains the insidious insight into his opinionated squib. He was one of the whiz-kids of the totalitarian Panchayat regime who was heralded for instilling the authoritarian element into that system. The King Mahendra, in his light mood, used to reckon him as one of the pillars of the Panchayat system. At this point of his career, when democracy is tottering, he presented himself as a true Machiavellian character because of his remarkable personal chemistry with the Palace. Thus, it is unrealistic to expect a democratic thought process from a die-hard Panchayati pillar that has a crypto-Marxist background.

In the political circle people are surprised about Minister Mohsin's discerning opinion and even more about the Cabinet's eerie mum. This is providing the chance to substantiate the long-standing quandary in peoples' mind about the independent functioning and executive authority of this government. No doubt, PM Deuba has a difficult task keeping his wonky coalition cabinet united, but this does not give his ministers licenses to act in an anarchic fashion. Minister Mohsin is not only a lone example of such flippancy;

the UML's ministers in the government are also behaving utterly in a style of *carte-blanche*.

Holding peace talks with the Maoists and the parliamentary election were the cardinal reasons for the UML to join the Deuba government. The Prime Minister seems pensive in declaring the election if the Maoists do not respond to his call for the peace talks. But the UML ministers and their leaders are in parallel contradiction as they are against holding the election unless the security situation improves. Amusingly enough, the UML, a major partner in the coalition, is neither preparing for nor in contact with the Maoists concerning the peace talks. Thus their vociferous demand for negotiation with the Maoists is a farce and is for public consumption only.

The UML has failed to keep the promises its leaders made to the public before joining the government. While talking loudly in public their ministers have truckled to many anti-people bills in the Cabinet. They do not have any explanation for their actions except their thrall to the chair. The frontline student organization of the UML and many top party leaders are criticizing their own ministers in public and telling them either to quit or prove their worth to continue in the present government. Looking at the plight of the UML somebody has rightly pointed out that this party is now tantamount to the Rayamajhi communists and that is why Madhav Nepal supports the anti-public statement of Minister Mohsin and does not smell rat in it.

If the Maoists are serious at what they are saying hitherto, then they will only talk with the one who wields the power. This suggests that they will not hold dialogues with anyone but the king. There is likelihood that the Maoists would not heed the Prime Minister's call for peace talks in order to demonstrate that they are not an easy push-over in spite of a recent serious military set-back in Pandaun in the far western region.

The UML is insisting that the Prime Minister Deuba hold peace talks instead of subscribing to his idea of going for elections. It feels unless the security situation improves, the said election would invite a gruesome bloodshed.

If the peace talks do not happen and election is not possible, what option is available to bring the country back onto the constitutional track and make people sovereign again? This calls for the attention not from the political parties only but equally from the king as well. As the King Gyanendra has on many occasions claimed that the Shah kings were always guided by peoples' wishes and people are watching him if he is serious to what he said about multiparty democracy and constitutional monarchy in his debut speech after becoming the king.

To bail the country out of the regression, the only peaceful alternative left is the restoration of the parliament. The Supreme Court should also show its prudence at this perilous hour rise above the nitty-gritty of legalities and justify its credibility. The government thus formed, will hold the election, talk with the Maoists and take up the issue of the constituent assembly also if so needed. Does the UML have the gall to quit the government and join the agitation in the Ratna Park again to demand the resurrection of the parliament? Or it should remain groveling at the feet of regression in the half corrected form? The UML has been caught between Scylla and Charybdis because of its double standard.

The Kathmandu Post – November 30, 2004

16

Leadership Conundrum in the NC

The Nepali Congress (NC) devoutly preaches what it does not practice. Power within the party flows down from the top rather than up from the grass-root level. This is the practice of the NC. It is diametrically opposite to the democratic dispensation for which it shows fervent conviction. The end result is, the party has emerged with only a singular leader. The NC, in its political odyssey, has had one family at its helm for over fifty years; that is, the Koirala family.

At present, three leaders from the second generation of the NC are talking about changing the leadership using their own version of justification. But looking at the confusion surrounding their ability to take rank in the party, once again, the leadership equation leads back to just one. It seems that the NC cannot think beyond Girija Prasad Koirala as its leader, but can Koirala think beyond himself? This is something interesting to behold in the upcoming general convention of the NC. The leadership Fahrenheit is at rise.

The octogenarian senior Koirala has led the NC for two stints as the elected president of the party but failed to redeem it to its past glory instead causing a devastating chasm. For better or worse he has run the party as a family enterprise, and therefore, feels privileged to bequeath its leadership to a scion of Koirala clan. From his point of view, if there is no acceptable candidate then he himself will continue. This is the rumor floating around spooking the party's political circle. Whether the rumor has substance or not, it will take time to reveal. But the political observers are astounded to hear the meek voices of Ramchandra, Shailaja and Sushil proclaiming that they would like to be the candidate for the post of the next president elect, only if the senior Koirala does not opt for the same. One wonders if these so-called leaders of the second-in-line are exercising their democratic rights or they are begging the president permission to contest. What an example of thralldom in the NC.

Everybody knows that the senior Koirala cannot be the party president for a third consecutive term unless the NC's rule-book is amended. Therefore, the NC observers desist to predict, observing that anything can be possible in the NC, if Koirala wishes it to happen. The name Koirala, after all, has become the synonym of Nepali Congress. The senior Koirala has run and shaped the party in such a fashion that, across the NC's political spectrum, one does not see the heir apparent, unless he is a genetic extension of the Koirala clan.

The second generation leaders in line are so pusillanimous that they prove as *en-fant terrible*. The Koirala overkill seems to have paralyzed the Next Generation of the NC. Within this grand old party of the country, politics has always remained as a family enterprise. Whether it is the Koirala in Biratnagar or the Giri, and the Nidhi in Janakpur, or Ganesh Man Singh in Kathmandu, and many others, the scenario is more or less the same with minor variations in the *cliché* ridden pretext. Being in political oblivion for more than two and a half decades, when the NC rose to power after the restoration of democracy, the temptation of the Me-Myself-I brand of politics is back again in the leadership. It has flourished in leaps and bounds when the leadership was handed over to Girija Prasad Koirala. He only seemed to be enamored with increasing the number of clan members and coterie rather than multiplying the number of stoic leaders. His leadership tenure proved a golden era for the henchmen. The multiplying number of clan members and coterie in the NC is seemingly a design charted out to subject the party to a dynastic functioning in the future.

The failure of the leaders of the second-in-line to deliver should be a cause of concern. There is nothing wrong to be loyal to the party leadership but one must keep one's self-respect. The three leaders, who have expressed their desire to run for the post of the party president, however, do not boldly declare that they would fight for the post; rather they seem to be begging for the generosity of Girija Prasad not to run again. What kind of leader will they prove to be, if elected, a pigmy president who will remain always under the spectre of Girija? Because of his tacit support for encouraging the cultivation of clan and coterie culture within the party, Girija Prasad is looked as a *bete-noire*. He is also blamed for the division of the NC, but he is still the president of the party. The NC is rife with the opinion that if he hands over the leadership to a new incumbent that will unite the divided NC. No doubt, it will be a desirable moment for sincere and true Congressites who are longing to see the NC united with the home coming of their comrades. But such unification without a moral ground always raises one question – How long will a party remain undivided when it is based on ego rather than ideological values?

After the demise of B.P. Koirala, the NC took refuge in three old men – Ganesh Man Singh, Kishunji and Girija Prasad. Ganesh Man Singh is no longer alive now, Kishunji, if not senile, is senescent and thus not active. This leaves Girija alone to continue the legacy of B.P. Koirala. Thus, in the NC, the next big question is, who is after Girija Prasad? The NC should be trying to remove itself from the Koirala rut and cultivating leaders who can inject inspiration to the party. Such dark horses exist; however, they are neither clan nor coterie to Koirala. And, therefore, it is hard for them to come forth to the front. The troika leaders who expressed their desire to be candidates for the post of the party president with condition Koirala does not run, are mundane and too servile. They do not command the respect of the cadre or the country. They have neither charisma nor acceptability. Thus, it is feared that their accent will lead to factionalism and disenchantment in the party rather than uniting it.

If the NC is to remain what it is today, when one looks at its leadership issue, the home-truth is, the party has stuck in a *cul-de-sac*: the only way to and from is the Koirala lane.

The Kathmandu Post – December 24, 2004

17

Pride and Prejudice

The nation was astonished when the Central Working Committee (CWC) of the Nepali Congress (NC) interpreted its statute, saying that Girija Prasad Koirala can contest for the post of party presidency for a third consecutive term, even though the rule-book does not concede. The rejoinder: the preposterous decision of the CWC is a vindication of charges that Koirala runs the party as his family business. Why not? After all, it is a country where family values come before national values. For some in the Koirala coterie within the CWC it was payback time, while for others it was a time of groveling. These sycophants have treated him as their indispensable leader. Despite the *cliché* ridden interpretation of the statute, there is not even a minute sign to justify that the wise men of the CWC, who took time off for the trend-setting meeting, have come away any wiser. They dare not rise above their servile behavior. The facile decision of the CWC reveals the desperate mindset of the titular CWC member seeking redemption in the Koirala surname. For these acquiescent Congressites the Congress dream only goes as far as the Koirala family. They believe that the NC can still go forward and remain united by riding on the jalopy of Koirala mystique. For them Koirala is both the message and the *messiah*.

Only one man in the CWC meeting refused to be carried away by the Koirala mystique, Ramchandra Paudel. He opposed the CWC decision by writing a note of dissent, though, timorously. He also must be blamed for the present predicament of the NC; because he did not put his foot down at the time when most of the leaders were busy enjoying the privileges of power rather than caring about the party.

Other CWC members, who posed themselves as maverick leaders, opposed the decision. However, after their tinseled sermons they came out of the meeting with their tails between their legs not even taking the time to put their disagreement on the record. Thus ends the grand drama of a party committed to instilling democratic values and culture in the country.

If there is one message that came loud and clear from this grand drama, then it is the NC that is Koirala's private enterprise and that he can extract any decision he wants from it. Furthermore, we should be ready for a few more nasty surprises from the NC in the future. One should not be taken aback if all the kith and kin of the Koirala family are elected/selected in the CWC in the forthcoming convention. In retrospect, the NC is recognized as a party of ideology. Kathmanduit leaders also have sacrificed their lives, when needed, for the cause of cultivating democratic values in the country. But after the restoration of multi-party democracy, when most of the time the NC was in power, Girija Prasad Koirala remained the leader. During these years the NC has been looked at as a natural ruling party of the country; however, it has gone from domination to damnation with many Congress leaders facing various corruption charges at present. It is no longer looked at as a party of ideology.

It has also lost its distinction of being a united party. Previously it was able to internalize its internal feuds and opposing views. However, it is no longer possible and a large vertical split has occurred. Thus, the word 'Congress' has lost its emotional edge and romantic psyche among the masses.

Nevertheless, the Koirala family is a hereditary glamour and a seminal idea for the NC because of the charismatic leader, B.P. Koirala. Some members of the CWC, therefore, still believe that the name Koirala ensures easy access in the minds of the common people and thus it is an acceptable and salable name. These subservient members tend to forget that a political party is like a swimming pool, if you don't change the water regularly, it will turn into a cesspool. Although, the Koirala family is basking in the past glory of the late B.P. Koirala, its angst is clearly visible as this family has no one else to hawk for the moment except Girija Prasad Koirala. He also wants to bequeath the leadership to one of his favorites while he is still active in politics.

Keeping this in view, he has shot a psychological salvo by asking the three aspirants who are striving for the leadership to come to a consensus agreeing upon a single name. All three are pushed-up leaders and Koirala knows that for them their egos are larger than the party; thus, they will never agree to accept one of the others as their leader. This provides Koirala a pretext to continue his leadership in the name of party unity. But for the political observers, this is only an interim arrangement until an heir apparent is decided in the Koirala family.

Koirala's genetic clan, be it Shailaja, Sushil, Sujata, Shekhar, Shashank or whoever it may be from this family, is suffering from crisis of acceptability. The latter three Koiralas are regarded as young leaders with unknown talents, since they have never been put to the test. The former two have squandered the opportunities to demonstrate their worth as visionary leaders in the party. Today, the NC is in a crisis. The need of the hour is to find a personality who is acceptable to the majority of the party cadres, no matter even if one happens to be from a senior or junior rank. Can Girija Prasad Koirala send this message out to the members of the forthcoming convention of the party? Will he take to heart the interest of the NC and save it from a Tsunami or will he be carried away by the dynastic impulse which would turn yesterday's pride of the legendry Koirala family to today's prejudice? The whole nation is watching.

The Kathmandu Post – January 18, 2005

18

Benefit of Doubt

The February First event, in the guise of the royal initiative, was in no way fortuitous, it was rather inevitable. And the inevitable has thus happened. However, this remains to be seen if this will work as an anodyne affair to the country's crises. But one thing is certain, it has relieved the people of unnecessary speculations and floating rumors. The reaction to royal action always enkindled love and hate within the public at large. This time, however, in between the two opinions there is a sizable proportion of tacit democratic supporters.

The country was facing political quandaries and was sinking into a blithering abyss of despair. Following the dissolution of the parliament two and a half years ago, all successive governments that were put on board, registered tall claims at the time of assuming the office, only to prove a damp squib at the end continuing to grapple with the Maoist problem.

It does not seem plausible that the bellicose Maoists, the bugbear for common people, are actually interested in resolving their issues in the interest of the Nepalis. Their despicable maneuvers are remote-controlled and guided from foreign lands in the name of international communist fraternity. Their lust to exterminate all opposition has incorporated savage means to such an extent that their cruel thought process remains no better than that of a Neanderthal man showing little mental development since the stone stage.

The concern of the agitating political parties against the regression is well-appreciated by the people; nevertheless, they have eschewed involvement in the agitation at large. This was a rebuke to the political leaders for their misdeeds. The people, however, still do not deny the political parties and, therefore, have never rallied round the extra-Parliamentary groups of right or left.

There was a stalemate in the country's political chessboard between the above political forces, while the entire nation was floundering. Under such a somber situation the king has enacted as a savior. In his long televised address to the nation he eloquently evinced his political savvy to tell the public that he is there in the time of need. However, his action whether right or wrong, will remain a topic for debate for a long time to come.

Now, the ball is in the King's court. If he is able to bring peace by resolving the Maoist problem and handover the power to elected representatives by holding an election within the time frame he has assigned for himself, it would vindicate his initiative of February First. The whole nation is waiting to behold when and how this will happen.

In an image-building effort, the King has recently spoken his mind to media, the first interaction since the February First event. He expounded upon his views explaining that the action he took was his compulsion and not a choice because of the grave and persistently deteriorating situation of the country. For political parties his action might look invidious, but Nepalis, at large, do not seem to doubt the king's intention and they are in a mood to give him the benefit of the doubt that he will restore peace and security.

In spite of peoples' verve to give the king an opportunity, the team he has put on board has disheartened his 'tacit supporters' and has also given his critics a chance to cast a doubt – Will the commitments he made in his address of February First be fulfilled? Particularly looking at the incumbents of the team, in the eyes of the Nepalis, some are notoriously famous for lynching the liberal and multiparty democracy in the past.

This time, however, the Nepalis were expecting that the king would give a chance to Meritocracy entrusting the job to maverick leaders. His Majesty, however, in cognizance of this concern assured the journalists that it is not the person who is important; rather, it is what he achieves. Thus, if the team's performance is not up to the expectation, this concern could always be raised again at a later date. This shows the pensiveness of the king and it is also a warning signal to the incumbents that they are there to achieve the objectives he has set forth in his address to the nation.

In the king's February address to the nation he highlighted the multiparty democracy as the polity of the peoples' choice and made a commitment to put the system back into effect as soon as possible. The address also provided a hope to build an understanding between political parties and him. As has been acknowledged by all, including the international communities, the country's spiraling Maoist insurgency crisis cannot be resolved either by military action or by the parties alone. And, thus an understanding between the king and the political parties is imperative so that the belligerent Maoists can be brought to the table. This is the point where all nationalist forces should converse, putting aside their party's interest. And, for this matter, the initiative should be taken by the King, as the ball is in his court now.

Our neighbors and the international donors can play a constructive role in mending the relationship between the king and the political parties. No doubt, their concern for multiparty democracy and constitutional monarchy in Nepal is well appreciated. Regarding this, the sooner these two constitutional forces are reconciled, the quicker democracy will be put back into place. The donors are resorting to aid cuts to press their point. But, they must remain mindful of the result of their action in the name of "restoring democracy." If they are not careful this kind of "economic terrorism" could hurt the vulnerable Nepalis and actually aid the insurgents.

The king in his interaction with the journalists has shown openness to his February action. In this light, the donors and the international communities, instead of looking for the punitive measures, should come forward with the suggestions that will help the reconciliation between the king and the parties. This kind of support will shorten the time in putting the derailed democracy back on track. Let the situation not develop as the proverbial saying – "when two elephants fight the grass is trampled always."

The Kathmandu Post – March 17, 2005

19

Chemistry and Politics

A hundred days after the royal action of February, in a *cliché* ridden approach, the government resonates in a high decibel alliteration of its achievements. The main stream political parties, however, haul the king's government over coals and dismiss all the claims stating that the political crisis in the country has further deepened bringing the country on the brink of a precipice.

The acrimonious arguments of both the government and the political parties remind us of the story of the four blind men who were given a task to touch an elephant and then describe it. The blind men described the elephant based on the particular body part they touched. Thus, each one's perception of the elephant was entirely different from that of his friends. Yet each was convinced that their limited view of the elephant was correct, that the others were perverse and untruthful.

The mouth-piece of the government, the Information Minister, Tank Dhakal and the leaders of the political parties epitomize the blind men of the parable.

The government is flaunting that after the February action, peace and security prevailed. While on the issue of bringing the dysfunctional multi-party democracy back on track, the government claims that its decision of holding the local body election is a step forward. However, to one's dismay the same election commission and security chiefs who were apprehensive about holding a free and fare election during Deuba's government now believe that the necessary conducive atmosphere has been cultivated for a free and fare election, even though, the Maoists remain unfettered.

The political parties not finding any changes to hold a free and fare election, deprecate the government's claim. In this grand political drama neither the government nor the political parties are taking the common people into their confidence, when both of them claim that they are working for common people, albeit.

The complex political scenario is difficult to comprehend in its entirety, particularly when the free press is restricted by the state under the pretence of the security. Political leaders and human rights activists, academicians and lawyers are still debarred from traveling freely, the only explanation given is "orders from up." Judicial orders are, by and large, either used by the government for its own convenience or defied without any retribution. The Fahrenheit of the rebels' presence outside Kathmandu is still very much felt. Under such circumstances opinions expressed by either party on the honey-moon period of this government remain imbued with many hues usually reinforced by political prejudices.

However, the fear has not, yet, been let up which is recently substantiated by the Maoists killing Shrestha and Sribastva – the coordinators designated by the government to the district monitoring committee of Chitwan and Kapilbastu. Again, in broad day-light when the military VIPs move through the street of the capital in security vehicles wailing sirens, this makes the common people feel how vulnerable they are.

The government cannot claim an unblemished record for itself either. It has remained highly intolerant towards press criticism and *laissez faire* for the free press is found only in the ministers' speeches. The human rights record of the country is at nadir. In Geneva, the International Community, therefore, passed Agenda 19 as stricture against Nepal. This is a matter of national shame for all of us.

Although the security chiefs agree to the point that the Maoist issue cannot be solved militarily, the government has failed to bring the rebels to the negotiating table. It indicates that the government also has no ace-card up its sleeves to resolve the issue politically. If this is the case, the government has no moral ground to blame the past governments for failing to resolve this problem earlier.

Above all, this government does not have democratic image as one of its vice-chairmen publicly utters that he does not believe in democracy. On another occasion, this wannabe do-gooder again spews his abhorrence saying that the king should not listen to (political) parties. If this is the hallmark of the government, how can common people trust that it will bring the derailed multi-party democracy back onto the track? After all, it must be noted that during the last hundred days, so far, the image of this government has not improved.

During the first press meet in the palace after the February move, while replying to one of the queries, the King had said that it is not who achieves but what is achieved – that is important. It is high time for him to monitor whether the performance of his ministers was commensurate with the assurances he had given to the people after his dismissal of the Deuba government a second time. The middle-class elites are watching him. His further actions will determine if they will go with him or elsewhere.

Kathmandu is a hot-spot for rumor. There is a fleeting rumor in the political circle that the king loathes the leaders of the political parties. The reason given is, it is chemistry rather than politics that functions more here. Although this rumor is rife in the capital, yet, the people want the king to prove it wrong by his actions, ensuring the passing off of the hundred days of his February move. Otherwise, the comrades in the jungle will benefit from the mess of chemistry and politics.

The Kathmandu Post – May 30, 2005

20

Government is Sleep-walking

For the last few weeks, the news related to Dr. Tulsi Giri, who took bank loan long ago and has not settled yet, has incessantly appeared in the various newspapers. Before the media broke this news, the government was preparing to bring a code of conduct, as recommended by a commission headed by the vice-chairman of the NPC, for bank loan defaulters. Ensuing Dr. Giri's name in the black list of bank defaulters, the government has remained eerily mum on the subject of the code of conduct due to be announced. Little wonder, if it spreads the impression around the world that abeyance of rule-book in this government is of common practice, when it comes for big-wigs.

Dr. Giri, currently one of the vice-chairmen of the Council of Ministers who has been claiming that there is democracy, does not seem bothered to take the people and the nation into confidence and clarify them about the accusation. Therefore, outrage spreads, news are posted, columns written, and e-mails sent. In the eyes of common people the government turns into a laughing stock with its credibility nose-diving.

In this mêlée, the government jumps to damage control in the mode of the government spokesperson Information Minister, Tanka Dhakal's harangue. During briefing to media persons he said that Dr. Giri is a respected person in the government and, therefore, he should not be slandered. The government has no knowledge if Dr. Giri has defaulted with a bank loan. If it is so and the bank refers the case to the government, it will do needful. What a ruse!

A news story appeared in the front page of *The Kathmandu Post* of June 25 as Dr. Giri averse to the NBL offer. The rejoinder: this government is sleepwalking... hence, does not hear the NBL's high decibel alliteration that Dr. Giri has defaulted the loan he had taken from the bank for the plastic company twenty years ago.

The entire drama is a *mea culpa*. And it reached its punch-line when it was revealed that he not only defaulted with the bank loan but his company has also not paid the taxes since its operation and the salary of the workers remains unpaid till date totaling to millions of rupees. Why does the Finance Minister dither to clear the code of conduct file, which is gathering dust on his table?

In a similar instance of defaulting with a bank loan a businessman was arrested recently in Biratnagar. But lately, the news is that Dr. Giri is negotiating with the bank to settle his loan in a concessional term. Does it not prove that the big guns are above the law in this land? If it happens, what will be the policy of the banks towards other defaulters now onwards? How will this affect the loan collection of the banks in future? The banks, a purely commercial venture, are forced to relive the thralldom of Panchayati era? The government is sleepwalking...., is there anyone here to listen to?

In a democratic polity, a person in a high public position is always answerable to the people and morally he cannot remain in that position unless he clears himself from the accusation labeled against him. This is a universal norm of democracy. But in Nepal it seems it is not accepted. As Dr. Giri is a hand-picked titular vice-chairman of King Gyanendra, he does not see himself accountable to the people, yet impudently enough he vaunts without compunction that he is here to serve the country. How would the civilized world take this tinsel?

The impression it spreads around the world is that in Nepal even one black-listed as a bank defaulter and has evaded government taxes for years willfully, he can walk away free and can hold a high public position as well. This ridicules the very essence of the King's desire of good governance and his search for leaders of clean image. The entire melodrama suggests that the system lacks public accountability and political openness.

Of course, corruption happens in democracy also but you cannot hide it because of the free press and the opposition, which are always on their toes watching the government if it is indulging in any wrong doing. If people do not say anything when their rights are curtailed by the government, it does not mean that they do not understand either. They wait for the right moment to exercise their power.

The euphoria of the February 1 move is slowly dying away as people could not see the promised change even after five months. The political stalemate between political parties and the King continues to deepen further. The government is not succeeding in bringing the Maoists to the negotiating table; except tall claims by the ministers who have tongue-in-cheek. The rebels are not showing war fatigue, which is proved by the recent attacks. Rabid conservatives are shoving themselves and flaunting their flippancy. The common people, therefore, are in apprehension that the anachronistic Panchayati order, which was rejected by 1990 revolution, is in reinvention.

People are dumbfound when they came to know that one of the royal choices has been black listed for defaulting with a bank loan. The King must be having a tough time in balancing the contradictions in the light of what he had promised to the people regarding good governance and eliminating the corruption at the time of dismissing the government of political parties and what one of the whiz-kids of his choice proved. People simply distaste Dr. Giri now. But the King's dilemma is he may not be enamoured to Dr. Giri, but it might be his difficulty getting a replacement that is a political basher and swears fealty too.

The Kathmandu Post – July 7, 2005

21

Revisiting Panchayatcracy

The King has not spoken his mind to the Nepalis *albeit* there are enough indications of what he is looking at. His each and every move is fraught with the desire of being the prima donna in political and state affairs. To achieve this end, he has to sideline the political parties and keep the Maoist insurgency bubbling up.

King Gyanendra has recently expanded his cabinet in the wake of continuous opposition against his government for its anti-democratic posture. A face-lift of the government was expected at home as well as abroad. But much to the chagrin of everybody, it showed that the King is enamoured of jingoes of Panchayatcracy and renegades who have pathological hatred for democracy and liberal polity.

If it propounds any message, it is this: the more the alliance of political parties, civil societies, rights organizations and the media brow-beat the King, the harder he bounces back. The King is not flinched from the discreet noises made by the political parties and the international community for reaching out to the political parties and settlement of the Maoist problem through negotiation. He is equally unperturbed even when the Maoists have forced their presence felt throughout the country by controlling countryside and whacking at any place and time they choose.

When the King took power in his hand, a sizable segment of the people hoped that he would steer out the country from the harrowing situation the country is facing. But even after the six-month hiatus, people could see no change in the gruesome situation.

When one looks at the faces of the incumbents in the government, the February 1 move of the King seems a kind of farce which was taken in the pretext of protecting the multi-party democracy and constitutional monarchy by establishing peace in the country. This move was an injury to the people of the country and democracy. To make the matter further worse, the persons inducted in his cabinet expansion – a convict, a by-word for hating democracy, and yet another bank defaulter – has added insult to the injury. Is it not indifference of the King towards common people?

Perhaps, the conservatives are elated by their success that helped the King empower himself. But in no way it is the victory of rabid conservatives, no it is not. Rather, it is a great defeat of political parties that made possible what was impossible a few years ago. The atavism vindicates that the orphaned conservatives did not melt in Fahrenheit 1990 revolution, but had just changed the color. Had those goblins of anti-democracy been arraigned, people would not have to pay the price for the mistake of the leaders.

The government is ambling into Panchyati polity. The politics of cohabitation has been pushed to the morgue, while the archival items like Dr. Tulsi Giri et al. are in revisit. The hubris of tap-dancing and servility are their hallmark and opera of decree is their parliament. Human freedom is banal for them while vassalage is emancipation. Yet they rant as wannabe do-gooders of people.

What the past six months have shown is that the King too could not rise above politics and prove himself as the tutelary of Nepalis. Thus, the monarchial infallibility has been subjected to public strictures marked by vitriolic language. Looking at the performance of his government till the date, people have felt that his commitments are only for convenience, not for democratic deliverance.

There has been no visible effort from his government except asking the Maoists to lay down their weapons before the negotiation. It is obvious, that, without confidence building measure, the Maoists will not put their weapons down unless they see that they are on the verge of defeat. They do not seem to be in such a predicament now.

Under such a situation, does the responsibility of the government end by just asking them to come for peace talks? It seems as if the royal government wants to keep this problem prevail so that the restoration of democracy could be delayed by blowing the phobia of the Maoist terror. Otherwise, there is no reason why the government is not opening other channels to pursue the rebels for negotiation, when everybody is saying that neither can win this war.

A new development is ensuing from the intransigent posture of the King in the body politics of the country – the political parties and the Maoists are getting closer to each other. Though it is too early to bet on it, but if they really get together, it is going to be quite difficult for the monarchy. This has already given shivers to the government. That is why, the information minister and the ex-chief of staff spewed antipathy against the alliance of the political parties.

From the interviews and the articles of ideologue, Dr. Babu Ram Bhattarai, it is becoming clear that there is a growing realization in the Maoist camp that the Arcadia of proletariat is unattainable at present. Their next stand now is for democratic republic or the election for a constituent assembly. From the people's point of view, the stand of the Maoists could be a negotiable point, but for the King and his government it is still too radical to think.

If the political parties are sidelined and pushed to wall, it is likely that the above two agendas of the Maoists could attract them for Armageddon, which will bring synergy between them. This will compel the King to talk either with the political parties or with the Maoists. Will it happen or how soon it happens is anybody's guess. Till then, the Nepalis should be prepared to pay more price for the lust of the King to rule the country by himself; be ready to enter the time tunnel once again.

The Kathmandu Post – August 8, 2005

22

Constitutional Monarchy

On a hot and humid day of 30 August 2005, Jawalakhel ground looked as if there was the Machhendranath fete sans chariots and devotees. However, it was the occasion of the inauguration of the belated 11th general convention of the Nepali Congress (NC). The government's faux pas decision to deny the BICC for the NC's convention brought it to Jawalakhel.

The open playground was jam-packed with the NC's leaders, foreign dignitaries, political observers, invitees and by-standers. The crowd was cheering their leaders to make the atmosphere lively and vibrant. At the one end, there was a raised podium with a back-cloth hanging on to which were a bust size paintings of the four leaders. Those who know the NC closely, it was a hypocritical kitsch of the party rank and file for, it is in no way close to the ideals of these leaders now. The eerie absence of K.P. Bhattarai, the lone living founder member, in the meeting evinces the mindset of the party establishment.

The entire country was looking at this convention. The youth and the new generation leaders were challenging the party rank and file to delete constitutional monarchy from its statute and go for a republican set-up. But, G.P. Koirala was giving controversial statements. The mercurial leader Shailaja was in support of the constitutional monarchy. She was of the opinion that it was not the constitution but the leaders who have failed to implement it in its true spirit. Therefore, the NC should not abandon the time-tested centrist line of the party. But her arguments did not gather much heat.

The NC is a party with inherent contradictions. The result of the presidential election in the 11th convention is the clear manifestation of the double standard of the congressites. In the closed door session the proposal for removal of the constitutional monarchy from the statute that was spearheaded by Narahari Acharya, one of the contestants for the President, was supported by an overwhelming majority, but in the election he was defeated.

The vote count (Koirala-1215 and Acharya-165) suggests that it is not the defeat of Acharya or his ideological stance rather it is the demonstration of congressites swearing fealty. This vassalage was further pronounced when more than 80% members of the old CWC were reelected. This has put the stamp on the NC that it is the party of a cult where dynastic overkill always works more than anything else. Otherwise, what is the rational for parading again the same pygmies who brought the party to this predicament?

The renunciation of the constitutional monarchy by the NC has a lot of suspense hidden in the text. The NC has to clarify its policy towards the kingship in the coming days. But if one delves into the past history of 55 years, one finds that the constitutional monarchy has had never been put into function.

Since, the establishment of democracy in 1951, no political parties had tried to institutionalize the constitutional monarchy in its true sense. The political parties squandered the Interim period (1951-1959) bickering with each other for being in power.

But, the King Tribhuvan and the King Mahendra had been wielding all executive powers rendering the cabinet merely an advisory body to help the King in ruling the country. Both the kings had curtailed the power of the Supreme Court (the then called High Court) by amending the Interim constitution when it clashed with their interest. The NC launched a *Satyagraha* in the winter of 1955 against the King's unilateral move when King Mahendra had to withdraw his order and agree to the six-point demand of the people. This victory of the people is known as the Magna Carta of Nepal.

In 1960, the first elected government of the NC lead by B.P. Koirala took the office. A new constitution was written, but it was drafted by the king's men. The army was placed under the command of the king. Clause 55 of the constitution was like the Damocles' sword hanging over the democratic force. Both the King Mahendra and B.P. Koirala looked askance at each other. B.P. knew his limitations with the king; nevertheless, he tried to keep him in good humor always by avoiding confrontation. In spite of his business acumen he could not avoid the inevitable. The result was the ambitious king dissolved the parliament and strangulated the democracy by using the clause 55 of the constitution. The constitutional monarchy was once again pushed into morgue. The king, thus, remained active for three decades.

People restored democracy once again in 1990. New constitution was drafted by the selected political parties. King Birendra, though with a pique, agreed to remain as a constitutional monarch. This constitution also did not assign army under the direct control of people's representatives. Therefore, constitutional monarchy during the twelve years of democracy was also not practiced in its true sense; rather, it was a pseudo constitutional monarchy in operation.

When the twelve years of democracy was defamed for its bad governance, people defended it saying that it is not democracy but the leaders, who are corrupt, need to be changed. Similarly, constitutional monarchy is never institutionalized and tried out till the date. So, would it not be a logical way first to think of a change of guard, rather than condemning the institution itself by asking to go for an alien system of republican set-up which we do not know how it will root in our soil?

Suppose, the NC with other political parties launches a movement for a republican set-up shunning the kingship. Will the extreme outfits of left or right, who have guns in their hand, not try to fill this power vacuum? Will the King not wield the military might as his last resort to meet this challenge, let alone the foreign interference? If this situation arises, can a country already shattered by the Maoist insurgency afford to go through another holocaust? All responsible Nepalis should think without being prejudiced. We have Pol Pot and Lalu Yadav as the example of People's Republic and Democratic Republic polity and we have Sweden and Norway also as the example of monarchy. Let us hope wisdom prevails over the leaders.

The Kathmandu Post – September 16, 2005

23

Gone to Kingdom Come

The afternoon walk of King Gyanendra was hailed by the official trumpeters as a colossal success. Why not? It has to be that way, as the servitude ministers and organizers of the walkathon have put their entire energy to make it a gala event. But the common people, at large, are blasé about the king's kitsch of winning people's heart. Has it helped to bring peace in the country or has there been any let-up in the misery of hapless denizens who are caught between the guns of two despots or has it allayed the angst of Nepalis or the international communities about democracy that is being stifled?

When the King was strolling with feline grace surrounded by security personnel, I was contemplating if there were an innocent lad of The Emperor's New Clothes parable amongst the orchestrated crowd to tell him the stark reality on his face. The interesting part of the royal walk was that the King wanted to present a soft image of him. Throughout his street walk he had worn a munificent smile on his face. He was patting school children and enquiring about their study, talking to elderly people, accepting flowers, *bintipatra* and waving to the cheering crowd. He also preferred this time a casual wear to military uniform. All this could produce somber effect only, when little tots were made there to stand from early in the morning only to be tired, exhausted and quite a few to be swooned. Was it an administrative terror or largesse of the government exchequer that has enticed the claque to flaunt? This was a general impression of common people about the royal walk apart from its political pay-off, if it has one, at all.

On the backdrop of the debacle of the king's failing to attend the UNGA meeting in New York, his street show was a damage control measure and to gain one's laurels. But political observers see, in no way, has it improved his sliding popularity. The sartorial affinity of his military outfits immediately overpowered him in his next visit to the western region diluting the soft image of the street walk of Patan. The common people have reason to believe it. On February First, when the King took over power the impression about him was not as it is today. People were of the opinion that it would create a space for something good to happen. But looking at the performance of the past nine months of his direct rule they clearly observe dichotomy of the said purpose of his takeover. People tend to believe now that either he squandered the opportunity he had grabbed or he has been forced by the rabid conservatives to go for Nepal-model of democracy, a second edition of Panchayat polity, which ultimately lands this nation to kingdom come.

The King's brinkmanship in international diplomacy has also suffered a serious setback as the country is forced to seclusion by our traditional donors. The assurances he has given to Kofi Annan, the UN General Secretary and the Prime Minister Dr. Manmohan Singh are seen nowhere near to be fulfilled. This has been taken as a breach of trust by the world communities. You cannot fool all the people for all the time; this is the opinion international community carry about Nepal now.

Following the audience to Lakhdar Brahimi, the special representative of Kofi Annan, the induction of another bank defaulter and a criminal accused in the cabinet in the same evening was a blatant rebuff to the international initiative, particularly of the UN, in resolving the Maoist problem and bringing democracy back on track. This is an indication that the King wants to deal with the country's problem on his own terms only. But things are not happening as he wanted, and he is aware of it.

The King is under constant duress to justify what he had done is correct. He appears to have taken too many opposing adversaries at a time. Fortunately, the army is still behind him and the political dispensation has not been able to grow real teeth to take on him. The Maoists are yet to prove that public allegiance and international support are behind them, *albeit* they control large part of the rural areas but with terror and gory acts.

Notwithstanding, the main threat to the king continues to be the political parties. It has the potential of creating an ambience that could lead to spontaneous spouting of common people on the street as in the 1990 movement. But the Narayanhiti is basking in the royal overkill that it believes will overtake the political party puissance under the putsch of a controversial RCCC and CIAA.

But the political savvy King Gyanendra knows that his hand-picked ministers are no match for the leaders of the political parties, if they have to face people. Because of their ineptness, there is a growing realization that the King has failed to deliver what he had promised to people in his February First address, despite his state power. People believe that his biggest failure is his inability to deliver peace and to engage mainstream political parties and the Maoists for a dialogue. This shows that the titular government has neither nerve nor vision up its sleeves to cope with the country's problem. This begets the King's critics to believe that his February First and then subsequent addresses are all promises but not promising enough.

When the King set out for cliché-ridden district tour, the helpless people everywhere requested him to bring peace and stability first so that the psychosis of fear could be replaced by the feel-secure factor among the people. But throwing cold water on the people's desire he announced the elections. No doubt, election is quintessence of democracy, but under the given situation possibility of a free and fair polling is more important than announcement. It is an open secret that the rural areas are under the dictate of the Maoists and they are boycotting the election. The voters will ruminate over the post-election security before they go for poll, unless they are forced to do so. Under such situation merely counting the number of security forces as ranted by the ex-army chief of staff is a fatuous optimism only to believe that it can provide post-election security. People simply do not buy it. The reason is, even though the security forces far outweigh the rebels in terms of number, training, equipment, logistics and resources, etc. yet, killing, abduction and coercion are a routine phenomenon in villages. Thus the ex-army chief's claim, if the number of RNA increases to 100,000 the election can be conducted, does not hold water. If election happens, as the government claims, without taking mainstream political parties, voters and, of course, the Maoists, into confidence, it will be an act of desperado on the part of the government.

Often the ministers and pro-election activists cite examples of Kashmir, Afghanistan and Iraq when people doubt on the possibility of holding poll under the present situation. Can one draw any parallel between Nepal and those countries in terms of (a) domestic support of the people and the political parties, (b) credibility of the incumbent government, (c) support of supper and regional powers, and (d) goodwill of international communities, to hold the election? Nowadays, election is not only a national affair; it is also an obligation of the host country towards international communities to prove it as a free and fair poll for its legitimacy.

Without creating a condition for peace and free media first, if election is forced on the people it will be tantamount to the Musharraf and Saddam Hussain style of election. The other possibility is, since the mainstream political parties and the Maoists are determined to fail the election, violence cannot be ruled out, ensuing *danse macabre* if wisdom does not prevail. The country will be drawn into the vortex of political crisis making it further vulnerable to the Maoists and foreign intervention. If such situation is not tackled with political acumen, the inevitable is knocking at the door.

The Kathmandu Post – October 31, 2005

24

Will Nepal Go Maoist?

Something peculiar is happening to the politics of this country. After the restoration of democracy in 1990, it was assumed that the country's politics had taken its final course and the political tug of war between people and the king had been settled for good. But the Maoist insurgency and the Narayanhiti massacre proved it wrong. The country has now become a hotbed for revolutionary political changes. Both the right and the left ultras are trying to establish a beachhead within the county's body politics.

There are serious concerns being expressed by the leaders of political parties, civil societies and world leaders regarding the threat to democracy. Practically both the extreme left and right are not very different. They both try to destroy democratic values, traditions, institutions and human rights, which were taking root in the country after the restoration of democracy. The defenders of democracy, therefore, need to ascertain from which direction, the left or right, comes the real threat to democracy.

The threat, of course, comes from both right and left extremes. If King Gyanendra means what he has reiterated in his addresses about democracy, although a large section in and outside the country do not take him at his face value because of his actions and the faces in his cabinet, it is less likely that the threat to democracy will come from extreme right even though the royalists and several cabinet members are openly flirting with fascist ideas.

Like many others, the US ambassador to Nepal, James F. Moriarty also regards the ultra-left as a threat to democracy. He apprehends that the Maoists have the potential to over-run the royal government and, therefore, suggests that the king should reach out to the political parties to resolve the current crisis. Let us try to enumerate the defenses that Nepal has against the Maoist totalitarian future.

The *first* defense is obviously the country's history. It is a comforting fact that no country having similar social and political history to Nepal has gone in Maoist's hand in South Asia yet. If we look outside the region to countries like Peru where the Maoist revolution reached its height, they have an entirely different historical and social setting. Twelve years of Nepal's democratic exercise has brought sufficient awareness in the people about the benefits of democracy, even though they could not be harvested fully due to the inept leadership. This could be the decisive defense against the Maoist takeover.

Similarly, even though the political parties may seriously differ in other issues, but they come together when a threat to multiparty democracy arises. The alliance of seven political parties at present is an example. However, with the democratic institutions weakened, fundamental rights eroding, political parties becoming increasingly unpopular and the sovereignity of the country coming under threat, a mere 12-year old democratic tradition cannot guarantee to counter the Maoist.

The *second* defense against the Maoist regime is that the Maoist is the country's most ruthless and bloody political group. Thus, it is quite unpopular among the people and its membership is lesser than what it claims. Also, the Maoists will not get freepost to score. It has to compete with various other communist parties who accept democracy and competitive politics. These parties can offset Maoists' strategy by offering better alternatives to the proletariats who are willing to listen. However, this does not mean that small number of cadres cannot hold back any party to take over the state power. The Bolsheviks in 1917 were also a small percent of the total population. But they managed to takeover.

Third defense against the Maoists taking power in Nepal is offered by the politically conservative nature of the Royal Nepal Army (RNA). Although this argument may sound superficial, it is true that Maoism has not penetrated into the rank and file of the army. The political loyalties of top and middle ranking officers are likely to vary from conservative to liberal democratic, but not far left. Apparently many, quite naturally as in most armies, have distaste for political leaders.

Yet another defense against a Maoist regime is the country's geo-political situation that prompts the concerns of our neighbors and international communities to ensure that Nepal remains a democratic country. The present world order is also against the Maoists, which does not believe in human freedom and advocates single party supremacy. Even though the Maoists cannot be defeated militarily, there is hardly any one who believes that their political revolution will be successful without goodwill and support of neighbors and major world powers. Such external pressure and synergy will remain as a strong bastion against the ultra-left advance in the country. Whether or not Nepal becomes a Maoist's 'people's republic' will largely depend, apart from the above mentioned factors, upon the people's wish to support the revolution. It is obvious that terror and intimidation alone cannot make a revolution a *vox populi*. Ultimately, they like anyone, have to win people's heart.

The Kathmandu Post – November 26, 2005

25

Squandering Ceasefire

There is one King Gyanendra, the one whom the seven-party alliance, civil society and rights activists love to hate. His direct rule of ten months is not something the country can be proud of. His royal government scored miserably low in democratic decencies, human rights dignities and political morality. And there is another King Gyanendra, a tough and efficient manipulator, who is resolute for peace and democracy as he has promised to his people.

But, paradoxically, it seems that he has got into a rut. Neither can he accept the ceasefire of the Maoists nor is he in a position to wipe them out. It is obvious that peace will not prevail here until the Maoist problem is solved. In spite of his soundbites, the truth is, he has been pushed to defense by the Maoists' ceasefire. It is interesting for the political observers to watch how he manipulates this predicament.

The Maoists' ceasefire has not only given sleepless nights to the royal government but it has also stolen the thunder from the king's claim of delivering peace by his government.

When the Maoists declared the ceasefire for three months, it was overwhelmingly received by all but the royal government. Although the government doubted the intention of the Maoists behind the ceasefire, yet no major incidence of violence has occurred during this period. Ironically, the royal government swaggered as if the returning of normalcy in the country is due to their security effort. Nobody is ready to buy this argument, as there are plenty of evidence that the Maoists have the guts and capability to waylay the government at any place and time.

The royalists, who are out to tap the nationalist instinct of people, went a bit too far with their intrigue making alliterating verbal attacks against the parliamentary governments of the past twelve years. Added to it the intransigent portrait of the king and his hubris to undermine the advice of the political parties, well-wishers and international community have created a space for the seven-party alliance to reconcile with the Maoists and the twelve-point understanding is the outcome. The unilateral ceasefire by the Maoists went off at a tangent swaying the king's position from a solution-seeking partner of the country's political crisis to the problem itself. This has brought reproach upon him, as people are tired of the senseless killings and displacement by the guns of both sides. They desire only peace, no matter where it comes from.

For ten-plus months the nation has waited breathlessly for the effort from the king and his government to bring peace and security by engaging the rebels in a constructive dialogue. But this did not happen. Much to everyone's chagrin the government spokesperson, Minister of Information Shirish Shumsher Rana has made it clear that the government would not reciprocate to the ceasefire but urge the rebels to take part in the municipal poll. This has made clear the mindset of the king and his advisors making it clear that the king is surrounded by garrulous hawk advisors who are less pragmatic and more dogmatic. It seems that these hawks still believe in violent solution by crushing the Maoists rather than going for a negotiated settlement of the problem.

Also disappointing was the king's address after Africa junket that failed to appreciate the attempt of seven-party alliance to bring the Maoist to an understanding for a broader interest of the country. He spoke about the scheduled election giving an impression that it is the panacea for all the problems.

No doubt, election is quintessential to democracy. It is not that the people do not support holding the election. The concern is, when such election should be held. For Nepalis, elections are product of peace, not a precursor to it. (Report of Greenberg Quinlan Rosner Research Inc).

Who are for the election at this moment? The hawkish royalists and jingo nationalists on one hand, and on the other hand, the renegades are supporting it. They look so servile that they took it for granted that the king's wish is people's wish; whereas in democracy it should be the other way round. Who are against the election? Everyone else. Even the supporters of the constitutional monarchy cast a doubt if election under such a situation is right. Thus, the election declared by the king is a political minefield where the royal government waxing inebriated with royal putsch is stepping on. What will happen is everybody's guess.

While speaking to foreign media at his office, the Minister of Information said that it is not the government that started insurgency and, therefore, there is no question of reciprocating the ceasefire. It is a very unfortunate remark and ominous sign for Nepalis. Surprisingly, the government seems to proffer the message to Nepalis to be prepared to undergo further hardship as this government is not yet ready to shun its obduracy to solve the Maoist insurgency. But the irony is even the military top brasses agree that this conflict needs to be solved politically.

There are examples that governments have agreed to release thc top rebel leaders to work out a peaceful solution. But this government is so insensitive towards the people's suffering. All indicators suggest that this hand-picked government is not interested in turning the ceasefire into an opportunity to find out a peaceful solution.

The Kathmandu Post – December 20, 2005

26

Electoral Rebuff

If one browses through the newspapers of the past one month, not a single address of Home Minister Kamal Thapa is without hate-blame-threat rhetoric aimed at the alliance of seven political parties, the rebel Maoists, civil societies, and civil activists. His recent outburst after the Tansen tragedy is a example of yet another, paranoia in his harangue to the press conference at the Home Ministry. Tell us Home Minister Sir, how many more sacrifices Nepalis still need to make to bring the country back to normalcy?

The municipal elections declared by King Gyanendra of his own volition turned out more as a game of royal ego than a democratic exercise. Even though the royal government has pulled its throttle full, the filling of nominations for only less than half of the total municipal seats by the candidates, that too with power calisthenics, proved it as a damp squib.

The royal government after losing people's faith is losing itself. The government is hell bent to conduct the poll, whereas the oppositions were dead sure to foil it. The entire nation is in funeral mood as people are apprehensive that if the hell will break loose in the aftermath of the election. But Home Minister, Kamal Thapa was distributing assurance of security, not only to the candidates but also to the voters, and would not accept the doomsday scenario; he is the chosen redeemer after all. In terms of credibility, the King Gyanendra's one-year direct rule has suffered several setbacks starting with the controversy over induction of tainted vice chairman and ministers in his council to African sojourn. Always credited with the successes and never held accountable for setbacks, the king's popularity has suffered miserably in the country as well as abroad after the February first takeover. The municipal elections which he has announced, of his own volition, became an object of derision when more than half of a little over four thousand total seats of fifty-four municipalities are not contested by any candidate.

In the past when there were elections, a deluge of candidates jumped in the election fray; compared with that standard this election proved a complete farce. Being a fatuous formalities, the funny side of this poll is, relatively a large number of candidates have been declared elected unopposed. Yet, the royal government is not prepared to accept the cold fact that the nonchalance of people towards the municipal polls is reduction and absurdum.

Apparently, the municipal poll has turned into a buffoonery when poll candidates are taking refuse in the administrative offices, the Royal Nepalese Army barracks or are being kept under tight security as prisoners as reported by several candidates themselves. Can it be called a democratic election in a civilized society by any standard? Will the elected candidates run their offices from the hideouts here after? The government is using the poll as a salvation politics, although it has turned out to be a worst-case scenario of political death wish.

Two home-truths permeate from the histrionics of municipal poll. *First*, people did listen to the clarion call made by the alliance of seven political parties to boycott the poll in order to register their disapproval for the king's action of February First takeover. In spite of perpetual bashing of political parties and their leaders in the guise of corruption and mismanagement by the royal government, people did not reject them not because they are enamoured of their leaders, but, because they know that these leaders could be removed if they commit mistake, while the king cannot be even if he does blunder.

It is, therefore, obvious that one cannot underestimate and marginalize the political parties if the political problem of the country needs to be addressed. In fact, people have proved that these mainstream political parties are kingpins in the body politics of a democratic country.

Second, the nomination of municipal poll has also debunked that the state television showing the footage of crowd swarming round the king during his districts' visits are not necessarily his supporters of February First action. The majority of them were claques and others were there out of curiosity and traditional respect. Had the majority of them been his ardent supporter the nomination for the municipal poll would not be so pathetic. It is, therefore, obvious that what is being briefed to the king by his ministers and rabid advisors is not what people desire. Hence, we see there is a clear mismatch between the king's action and the people's wish. Without playing any blame game King Gyanendra needs to revisit his actions if he sincerely cares for the people's wish.

The government may declare whatever result they like of the municipal poll but people's reluctance to contest in this poll show that their priority is not the election. In their agenda 'peace' tops the list. But peace cannot be established in the country until the Maoist problem is addressed. Till date, there has not been a sincere attempt from the part of the government after February First takeover in resolving the Maoist problem because of its cocky nature, which is costing the country in terms of national economy. Now it is up to the government prudence if it listens to the bark of the oppositions or waits for the bite.

The Kathmandu Post – February 14, 2006

27

Dialogue: Missing Link

For people who believe in teleology, our epics are full of mythological metaphors to represent them and here is one straight from the classic *Mahabharata*. King Gyanendra, it seems, has turned himself into the tragic warrior Abhimanyu trapped by his own opinionated mannerism. His message on the occasion of 56th Democracy Day reveals that he is floundering yet; whereas people are blasé about his one year of direct rule.

The Democracy Day should have been an appropriate occasion for the king to show deference to people's wishes in order to salvage the country from the political quagmire.

There are moments in the history when the unrivaled rises up from the predicament looking different and talking different. But the sacrosanct monarch, frozen in the royal atavism, was dusting up tinsel from the past with full of platitudes and generalities. The phraseology did not instill any plan to cope with the changed realities which everybody is talking about; rather, it was like discovering the history once again forgetting the present. Political observers reckon that the king has missed a chance of reconciliation thereby making him responsible singularly for the *status quo*.

On the backdrop of the SC verdict on the RCCC and the constitutional limitation of the king, the king's message on the Democracy Day failed to send ripples within the political circle and outside. Never before, a towering institution of Nepali unity had looked so mundane because of *mea' culpa'*. His rabid advisors and servile vice-chairmen and ministers, who are the most indulged synonym for the pathology of power, are no less responsible for the predicament. These sycophants cannot think beyond the king; but can the King Gyanendra think beyond himself?

The King Gyanendra, who is popularly known for savior faire, should show sagacity to roll back on the decision he had taken on February 1 on the ground the judgment passed by the SC on the royal prerogative and his constitutional limitations. This will evince his political savvy and hopefully lift up the image of the crown that is on slide. It will also provide a vent to the impasse that presently exists in the body politic of the country. The sooner it is, the better it will be for the people and the country. Let us keep our fingers crossed that the *tête-à-tête* the king is having at Pokhara will precipitate to a much needed full blown dialogue with all concerned.

Apparently, in his message of the Democratic Day it looks that the king has made a call on political parties for dialogue but there is a qualifier attached to it – interested. The royal call may sound music to the ears of the servitors but the qualifier connotes that the king is seemingly bent on talking to the political parties of his choice.

As the capital is rife with rumors, one should not be surprised if these 'interested' are fringe political parties only. And interestingly, these parties wax visible and heard only at the time of election. The mass contact of these political parties does not extend beyond the corridor of the party office. Talking to such parachute political parties would prove nothing but an event of inanity, which is tantamount to beating around the bush. The mainstream political parties have ruled out the dialogue with the king until he resurrects democracy. Under the situation the king has a challenge to prove the rumors false by rescuing his dialogue-initiative from being sabotaged by the royal hawks. He looks politically so isolated that he has no one with him who has a skill and charisma to give it a push, *albeit* too many spoilers around him.

Ever since King Gyanendra has his tryst with history on February 1, major political parties stopped believing him at his face value. The king's Democratic Day message came as yet another example that vindicates their stand. Paradoxically, his kitsch of reaching out to political parties for dialogue has excoriated his mindset when he extolled the recently held municipal polls, widely criticized as a farce inside and outside the country, as a triumph of democracy. This has created a distrust of the king among the parliamentary forces as there is no effort being ever made by the royal government for confidence-building measure (CBM). In the absence of such CBM the king's call for dialogue has turned into a placebo.

It is obvious that the one year of direct rule of King Gyanendra failed to deliver what he had promised in his debut address-to-nation at the time of the usurpation. His business acumen also could not pull back the country from the brink of a failed state and thus the nation finds itself at a critical crossroad. Taking correct decision and at the right time is key not just for business corporations but for the nation as well.

For this, one needs to be rational and not emotional. The king should stop thinking the political parties as red-rag and the rebels can be controlled by military might. One should not hesitate to lend ears to his adversaries as well when the issue demands national consensus.

In the Democracy Day message his holding of fig twig if it purports the inner conscience of King Gyanendra, let us hope prudence prevails. At the serene and salubrious surrounding of the Phewa Lake where the king is retiring, he should do some retrospection. The profound vastness of the Phewa that leads one to mystic enchantment when he beholds it from its bank overwhelms the petite ego of the mortals – 'be it a monarch or a mendicant.'

The Kathmandu Post – March 7, 2006

28

Que Sará Sará

The more it covers, or pretends to cover, the more it gets exposed. This is the story of this government. He may say it all about security concern feigning the Maoist infiltration into the valley in the foretold four-day peaceful strike of the Seven-Party Alliance (SPA). But, in practice, it is about the denial of the constitutional rights of the SPA under the pretext of various jargons of law and order.

Home Minister, Kamal Thapa, behaving as the supreme arbiter of Nepali destiny, is flaunting his conjectures as always right and just. His edict, coming in alarming frequency as the SPA movement is zeroing, is an indication of how intolerant the regressive government can be lest the democratic wave similar to that of 1991 movement reappears. Such populist style of politics can hardly be considered unwarranted in a democratic dispensation as compared to the continuing failure of the non-popular government to create popular consent at the time when the parliament is stiffled. His edicts to the SPA are to roll back from the 12-point understanding with the Maoists, or else be ready to be treated as terrorist, withdraw the announced peaceful strike, or else be prepared to face curfew and arrests. The government has further plans up in its sleeves – declaring state of emergency, closing telephone, mobile phone and newspapers. So much so the government has warned public not to travel to the capital and has turned the valley into an island by blocking all the vehicles coming to it.

He is the vestige of the Panchayati autocracy, yet ironically flaunts about democracy and claims that his security concern during the SPA strike is at people's behest. What else could be the cruelest irony?

Honourable Minister, we are in 2062 BS and this is not an ancient time. People of 21st century are not Neanderthals. You can't fool them by your banal comments made regarding the ceasefire announced by the Maoists in the valley. Ceasefire anywhere anytime is a matter of relief for common people living under constant threat of guns from the both sides.

Today, the movement of democracy is so heated up that the vestiges of the Panchayati autocracy are incapable of continuing the game. For, it was not long before when such *betê-noires* are on the run and subterranean immediately after 1991 movement.

But, at present, they are vaunting as the most privileged custodians of democracy and the word democracy has become their war cry.

History tells us that great nations are those which are led by great leaders and they are always popular among common people. But those who acquire power without a popular mandate always fail to win the hearts and minds of common people. This is what King Gyanendra is facing today. There is a wide chasm between what the king thinks and what people feel.

Common people, time and again, have made the wanderlust king aware of their jeremiads and overwhelmingly expected him to bring peace and security, because they sincerely believed that he could deliver it if he wanted. Instead, the king proffered a farce of municipal poll, which was rejected by a large majority of people.

Given the *faux pas* offer of the king, the opposing political parties got another opportunity to pick a fight with the government. The king and his government seem not to take heed of public disenchantment and determined to indulge in yet another election sometime next year. This reflects that the king gives pittance to the public opinion and wants to go ahead with his road map, on which no public opinion has ever been solicited, giving an impression that no matter *que sará sará.*

In politics, one capitulates only when he is totally vanquished. As everyone accepts the king (K), political parties (P) and the Maoists (M) are not in win-win situation. Yet, the government is lackadaisical in creating conducive climate to bring the other two sides on a negotiating table.

Political stability in the country can not be guaranteed unless the Maoists are terminated or brought into the mainstream. The SPA has meticulously worked out 12-point understanding with the rebels in order to bring them into the mainsteam. The credit of Maoist ceasefire in the valley goes to the Maoist. Baffled by the offbeat step of the rebels, the belligerent Home Minister has become less pragmatic and more dogmatic in his comment about the ceasefire.

The hawkish government, which believes in the policy of hot pursuit and bringing the rebels to heel, is always at alert to grab any situation that pushes the negotiation further away. Since the life of the government depends inversely on the understanding reached among the political forces K-P-M, the government is trying to prove that the SPA movement is being manipulated by the Maoists to perpetrate violence. But nobody believes it in the light of ceasefire declaration by rebels.

The government is determined to exploit the predicament to the hilt so that the gap between the king and the SPA would widen, freezing the chance of immediate dialogue. In spite of facing the peaceful demonstration with democratic moral, the government is looking for a pretext to suppress it by force, no matter what repercussion is unleashed, *que sará sará*.

The Kathmandu Post – April 7, 2006

29

Don't Repeat the History

Yesterday, if the king raised his eyebrow against any leader, the latter was either sacked if he was in the cabinet, or put behind bars like the then Prime Minister Sher Bahadur Deuba. Today, if anyone talks on the street in favor of democracy, it is the king who catches fever inside the Narayanhiti. He starts consultations with political doctors – the plenipotentiaries of India, China, USA, former PMs and leaders of the political parties.

In the fourteen months of his direct rule, the king failed to deliver what he had promised while taking power in his hand. Gone are days when the king and his nominated vassals were the sole arbiter of destiny of the Nepalis. But the king failed to read the writings on the wall either because of his obduracy or the vested interest of his servile advisors. In either case the blame solely rests on the king himself. Today, his vocal supporters have run out of steam and are seen nowhere around to stand by him. He is there as a lone monarch isolated from all around, which is the price of his brinkmanship.

Judging by the controversy the king has instilled by his February 1, 2005 move in its current context, it is not difficult to arrive at the conclusion that usurpation of power by him gave very little advantage to the king and the institution of monarchy at large. In front of the people's wish the wannabe good-doer king could not stand by his words and his action proved to be Achilles' heels. This was king Gyanendra's first tryst with totalitarian temptation. He wanted not only to be 'seen' out be 'heard' as well.

On the 19th day of peaceful movement of people called by the Seven-Party Alliance (SPA) had drawn the attention of the world. As per the 12-point understanding between the SPA and the Maoists, the latter also actively cooperated in the movement along with the civil society activists, rights activists, professional organizations and people from various walks of life to make it a success, *albeit*, the government goaded the Maoists to make it a bloody one. But they refrained from violence. This was a praiseworthy step on the part of the rebels.

But, on the other hand, the success of the peaceful movement must have ripped away the delusion of the Maoists that power can be transferred only through guns – a weird dogma for 21st century. Will the bellicose Maoist leaders take notice of the writings on the wall? Their armed revolution of more than a decade has proved to be fruitless? Rather, it has instilled unprecedented misery and damage.

Some of the so-called human rights elites with skewed vision are making facile remarks on public platform that the success of April 24, 2006 is not because of the peaceful movement but because of the decade old armed revolution. If this is the case, what were the Maoists waiting for the last ten years? The accolade for the Maoist by the egalitarian rights leader is a *non sequitur*. Such indiscreet expression should be regarded as analogous with sycophancy and will not encourage the rebels to drop their arms and renounce violence – a major step for peace negotiation. Yet, one should not underestimate the contribution of the Maoists' armed struggle in setting the stage for the movement.

Of course, the leaders of the SPA have made a blunder by not taking one of the allies of 12-point understanding into confidence, but does it mean that one should close one's eyes from the truth? The rights leader's statement is an affront to the martyrs who had sacrificed their lives for the cause of the movement.

He is the leader who is the most indulged synonym for pathology of double standard when he had fought the election from the capital under the symbol of the CPM-UML but introduced himself as an independent candidate. What a ruse!

The peaceful movement supported by the Maoists as well has created a new political mainstream in the body polity. The three months of ceasefire announced by them is a welcoming move but it is not sufficient enough a proof to believe that it is a real change of heart. If they really believe in people's power, it is time for them to come forward to participate in the competitive politics and stop threatening with the might of their guns.

Everyone acknowledges that the parliament, which has been restored because of the people's movement, is there for a specific purpose which is to address the issues raised by the movement, i.e., to go for constituent assembly and restore peace by involving the rebels. Under this backdrop, the negation of the parliament restoration by the Maoists raises a serious question on their intention to join the mainstream politics, when their political constituency does not extend beyond their terror factory. They should come out of the beaten path of the Bolshevik psyche that one who is not with us is against us and can be disposed off violently. In democracy, such outlandish opinion is always wrong. When you are wrong you cannot be right.

Comrades, have courage to face the people's verdict. If you have done good to common people, they will welcome you like heroes; but if you have harmed them, they will decide accordingly. Remember many revolutionaries, powerful emperors and despots have gone down the dark lane of history when they failed to read the aspiration of their people. Let us hope that you will not repeat that history.

The Kathmandu Post – May 9, 2007

30

Will the Left Act Right?

Nepalis have done it again and surprised the world. The phoenix of democracy has stumped political observers and also proved the Shah kings' rhetoric wrong that they have been reining over the country according to the wishes of people. It was not so; the April revolution was the testimony of the fact. The accidental king Gyanendra who was considered ostentatiously popular and entrenched has been forced by that revolution to capitulation of the usurped power to people again. The king taking refuge in the fantasy of the myth of the Shah dynasty had taken the country for granted and failed to read the popular mind. In the quest of proving himself the sole arbiter of Nepalis, the royal hubris turned him so indiscernible that by the time the people's tsunami became an awesome reality and remained no longer a metaphor, it was too late for the king to undertake any damage control. Today the 237 year old monarchy has turned into a worst-case scenario of its own death wish.

Along with the shattered crown, there is a new iconography of the SPA, *albeit* the faces are not so refreshing. The SPA leaders stood tall and tried to look sagely only to reveal their true colour, be it Pradeep Nepal of the UML or the leaders of the PFN or the Sadbhavana Party or both the Congresses, at the time of distribution of ministerial pie. Further, the SPA leaders' pent-up pathology of distrust of woman leadership was proved to the hilt, when they failed to select Chitralekha Yadav as the speaker of the House. This insinuates that the mindset of these loquacious leaders is no better than misogynists.

But the canvas is not complete unless a new icon which is known for his medieval brutality and terror for a decade is taking a space; rather, he has colonized the political space. And, he is the Maoist chieftain Prachanda, who was till yesterday a most wanted man by the State and the Interpol. He is today a most awaited man to be seen. His party is only a decade-old but it is fraught with a mega ego of being a *messiah* of downtrodden following an outlandish ideology of the Maoism which is looked as a misplaced slogan in the context of today's world order of globalization. Under such paradoxical predicament, one does not need to wait for aeons to see if their ideology would turn into Achill's hill of Prachand doctrine, unless they instill reforms in the party line as demanded by the time. Otherwise, the saga of Rabindra Shrestha – Mani Thapa will not remain as sporadic incidence.

Every Nepali is keeping his finger cross for the safe landing of the Maoists in the country's mainstream politics. The recently signed eight-point compact between the government and the Maoist is a step forward in settling the political confusion that had cropped up after the reinstatement of the parliament. Further, the adjournment of the House for 17 days is yet another positive step of the government to take the Maoist into confidence. With all these positive vibes, there are some gray areas one beholds in the Maoist court. The extortion spree, termination of one who does not acquiesce with them, intimidation of media, violation of human rights, etc. are the dark spots on the canvas which are difficult to condone.

The Maoist cadres are yet continuing the above heinous acts under the nose of the leadership and till the date there is no indication that they have been enjoined restrain from holding such acts. This brings two messages out in public. Either such extra-judicial acts are continuing under the espousal of the leadership or he does not have control in the party rank and file *in toto*. Continuation of such ambiguous situation does not help the leadership to keep sustain public sympathy for long. At the time of the election of the CA their manifesto and the tall talks only would not buy them support. People, without doubt, will rake up their past in order to be assured that this will not continue in the future as well. Here Prachand is on ordeal as, till the date, the deeds of the opinionated cadres do not match the words of their leaders.

Now-a-days, we are coming across within the newspapers and interviews, all sorts of explanations by the Maoist leaders justifying the illegal acts of extortion and abduction. If it is a just act and they think that people should also support it, why they dare not include them in the 12-point and 8-point compacts as well as in the code of conduct they have signed with the SPA and the government? The political savvy Maoists know that such acts are illegal and cannot be justified in any civilized society and, therefore, resort to brandishing the hubris of gun power. But one should not forget that people in democracy take notice of everything. Thus, if the Maoists' booty boots them out from national scene one day, one should not be surprised.

In open politics, if the violation of human rights by the security forces is a culpable act, no doubt, the atrocities in the past and the present, perpetrated by the Maoists are also akin to such violations. No amount of self-criticisms can absolve one from punishment when both the warring parties have knowingly or unknowingly violated such rights repeatedly. Under such situation, if only one party is subjected to scrutiny it will inculcate a culture of impunity in others legitimizing all their crime in the name of people's war.

No doubt, the Maoists have to feed their cadres who are the PLA and militia and so have other political parties their members, like the Maoist cadres, who are also the frontline workers of their parties. If these political parties also resort to extortion in the pretext of feeding their members or else demand with the government to make provision of budget for sustaining their members, what will the government look like? Will the donors remain mute and continue their support? This suggests that the Maoists are in habit of volition to get things easily in the name of people's war. What can you call it but a *Veerappan* Culture?

A party with a difference, as its leaders claim, which was subterranean for a decade now seems restless conjoining the government. This is the impression one gets from the statements and interviews of the various Maoist leaders. So much so, in Parbat, putting all the norms of democracy in morgue, the Maoists took over the chair of the DDC president on its own and announced *fatwa* as well only to renounce when their *faux pas* was fiercely censured from all political quarters. This has raised a serious doubt on Prachand's vaunting of accepting the competitive multi-party system, where as his cadres still maintain the mindset in period costume and *ante di luvian* dogma of barrel of gun.

Once they become the part of the interim government, it will be interesting to watch if the Maoists will look at the issues from open society perspective or from the law of jungle which they are used to?

The Kathmandu Post – July 7, 2006

31

Monkeying Around with Peace

Last week, when the NC, the UML and the Maoist leaders sat in conclave at Godawari Village Resort, the other partners of the SPA were miffed at being kept out of the loop. There was hue and cry raised in the cabinet and the ministers demanded that the talk team should brief the proceedings of the Godabari meeting to the cabinet. The spokesperson of the NC (D) Minendra Rijal was so annoyed that he branded the high drama as 'snooty' (*TKP*, July 17, 2006).

But when the scheduled summit talk between the SPA and the Maoist leaders deferred without another date being fixed and the government's letter written to the UN was released by the parliamentary committee, on both the occasions there was discontent writ large on the faces of the Maoist leaders, but they could sent out only mixed signals of objection and cooperation but no confrontation. In the three months of their overground relive, the Maoist, of course, see no contradiction in running with the hare and hunting with the hound.

This Maoist atavism, if it sends any message out loud and clear, it is how desperate they are to enter the government. If this is the case, their tall talks about the common people's concern and welfare are but the rhetoric. If not, why the Maoists, even for once, dare not ask people if they should join the government at this stage or they should wait till they get people's verdict in the CA?

When we hear the philo-media Maoist leaders talking their policies about industry, tourism, FDI, agriculture and land reform, private property and the role of private sector, Nepali semi-skilled labour in international market, human rights etc. in TV, it seems as if they are lecturing freshmen or their cadres. They can not think beyond the beaten path of outlandish communist ideology which is a weird idea in the today's world order of globalization. How one could attract foreign investment in the country when intimidation, extortion and labour imbroglio, in various pretexts, are in perpetuity for political gains. Land reform for them, it seems, has not moved beyond their cliché-ridden rhetoric – land to the tillers. To this effect, they have no new and innovative ideas to offer except distributing land to the landless, without taking into consideration the ensuing production loss, for their political benefit. Regarding private property and FDI their ambiguity comes on the surface when one reads the contradictory statements of the top leaders.

While rhapsodizing over the Maoist hyperbole one should not tend to condone the neighbouring Indian state West Bengal which is under the reign of the communist party for last twenty eight years. It has done little for the economic salvation of people and state in general. In the ranking of the twenty big states it is always below half way mark in the rating and in the year 2004 it has slipped to the fourteenth position from twelfths (*India Today, August 16, 2004*). Today, West Bengal has been proved as a saga of economic atrophy; how can the Maoist assure that Nepal would not suffer the same once they join the government? As the credibility of the Maoist has lost much of its heat in the three months' time of their overground activities, when people saw a wide gap between what the leaders say and the cadres are doing in the districts. They expect all others to abide by their rules (nowhere written) but keep themselves above the rule of the state.

Here comes a letter of Prachanda to Annan much hyped by media with a big bang. No doubt, the government's mannerism in the peace process, be it the letter written to the UN or be it the Godawari conclave of three parties, is not free from censure. It should be the duty of the government to take the rebels into confidence and must not act unilaterally, if the broader goal of the CA election is to be achieved. But this does not mean that the Maoists need to behave recklessly, because they are rebels. Otherwise, everybody knows that unless the government, the SPA and the rebel agree the UN can not start their mission of arms management. Therefore, the points raised in his letter by the rebel chief to Annan could be amicably discussed once the UN team arrives here. Under such situation what purpose the letter would serve other than a spoiler giving an impression that the parties are fooling each other and not serious in the peace effort.

Instead of behaving as a cry-boy, Prachanda could have used the opportunity to suggest some doable apple-card, so that it is a win-win situation for all. May be it was politically imperative to write the letter, but in essence, one feels many elements of hubris in it, such as, the proletarian arrogance, the awareness of its military might, the sole arbiter of Nepali destiny and self-righteousness with which for past one decade they have been subjugating people to their decisions unilaterally.

Prachanda's odyssey has gone through many ups and downs and finally has arrived at the door-step of peace. One gets surprised at how a political savvy, the rebel leader, allowed himself to be manipulated and manoeuvred by the hawkish Maoists who tried to push 'the peace', which is tapping the door, further away? He should not let the ordeal, he passed through, be wasted for the interest of a few hawks. The letter written by the CPM-UML is still live in the memory of Nepalis like a nightmare, because of which the World Bank has put a much ambitious the Arun Valley Project in the cold box. What benefit the UML has got except its cocky ego satisfaction at the cost of the country's development and economic progress of the people in general? The UML was then excoriated extensively for its wannabe do-gooder role, which Nepalis prefer to call monkey-behaviour, as the country had lost a huge opportunity of economic development.

The way the government is acting, it was a natural reaction by the rebel chief to write the letter to the UN to register his objections. Let us hope that the present epistolary started by the Maoist chief does not abort the conducive atmosphere that has been created to bring peace in the country. We like to be surprised once a while that the Maoists will prove it wrong that the monkey-behaviour is not a generic mannerism associated with communists.

The Kathmandu Post – July 29, 2006

32

The Red Alert

The peaceful April revolution demonstrated the zenith of understanding and cooperation between the SPA and the Maoists, forcing the King Gyanendra to hand the usurped power back to the people. After four months, however, the SPA government and the Maoist relationship hit a nadir. The rebel leaders overtly demonstrate their frustration by flaunting hyperbolical rhetoric claiming to start a similar revolt as the October Revolution if their demands are not met. They have said they will not return to the jungles to fight, but will encircle all of the major cities, claiming it will be a peaceful revolution. Nobody, however, is willing to believe them, as the Maoists, regrettably, remain reviled figures among the general public with their demonic acts of the past, while flippancy and hubris are still their statesmanship.

When the Maoists joined the April revolution, spearheaded by the SPA, many believed that peace would prevail in the country. Commentators were quick in their predictions that once the rebels joined the interim government, everything would become normal in the country. Soon they were proven wrong. The SPA government turned volitional and left the rebels kicking their heels, while the Maoists were vitriolic from the first day the SPA government took office. Occasionally, the SPA government riposted, thus both look askance at each other.

If the Maoist rebels are able to make people believe that their perception and intrigue can accommodate competitive multiparty democracy, then Prachanda's posturing and interviews with the BBC and Dr. Bhattarai's recent statements about India and America are seemingly right.

How come, suddenly, the expansionism and the imperialism, which have remained for so long the dirtiest imposition that the Maoists, for that matter all Nepali communists, are raging against, have become an acceptable face for the rebel leader? Is it change of heart on the part of the brazen dialecticians or that Moriarty and Shiv Shankar have prevailed on them? Apart from the tinsel, there is nothing that proves they are trustworthy of their eulogy.

Inspite of the euphemisms used by both the SPA government and the Maoist leaders, the *mise en scène* has changed very little in terms of the seminal issues of decommissioning weapons, the restructuring of the state and the monarchy in the interim period. With several high profile consultation stints, now the rebel leaders seem cognizant of the home-truth that with their cocky ego they can go nowhere near the gallery of power. And if they want to be in the Singhadurbar, then they need to make compromises with their *ante-di-luvian* policies in period costume and be able to live with withered and dented egos. How the indoctrinated comrades, who are brainwashed to believe in the dreamland of their dogmatic philosophy, will react to the situation?

Now it has been evident, without going through compromises the rebels will not be able to participate in the government. This is the leviathan dialectical dilemma the rebel leaders are facing ever, where they need to save their bastions and support the SPA government as well. The pervasive attitude and the excoriating statements of the Maoists are the sharp reminder of this complexity. The Maoists' perceptions of the SPA government are deeply ambivalent. They disparage but admire; they resent but expect jealously with a desire to emulate. Such split psyche has caused to their image of do-gooder more harm than good.

Maoist leaders, in the party, are trying to balance militarism and political maneuvering at parallel, *albeit*, the former dominating most of the time. Under such situation, if the leaders go off at a tangent, it certainly would give sleepless nights to the hardcore comrades. The changing views of the rebel leaders show these contradictions.

Joining the government and cohabiting with the SPA partners might be a power sharing for the leaders at the centre, but for the ideology-harden comrades it is like sleeping with the enemy. How the comrades at grass root will reconcile with this 'principal contradiction' will be an interesting phenomenon to be watched. If the spectre of Mao haunts them as a ghost story, remains to be seen.

If history is a guide, Prachanda's ordeal has only just begun. He has to placate his highly charged, self-styled vigilantes and at the same time balance the glaring contradictions within his party, as well as with the SPA. If the see-saw goes out of balance, his troubles could begin from nowhere else but right at home. This looming situation is being anxiously watched by political observers. Whether he can prove himself a consummate leader, only time will tell. But he has begun a trek, which can only be said, will lead to the political minefield where termination is a Hobson's choice, when one fails.

Conceit and double standard of the Maoist rebels continue to come visiting us showing different faces of Machiavellian character, no matter where we are. Defying every norm of statehood, they behave as a state within the state, forcibly collecting taxes in the districts vaunting as they are the government. But, recently, when Mahara traveled to the UK, he uses the passport issued by Nepal government and not the one issued by the government of his party, which they claim it is running in the districts. Does propriety means anything to these Maoists? Is it not a moral bankruptcy and double standard on the part of such leaders?

We saw such uppishness in Baluwatar on the way to the PM's residence where the flippant cadres of Prachanda took the street virtually under their siege feigning the security of their leaders.

If the PM's official residence is not safe for the Maoist chieftain, where else on the earth will he be safe?

Also the arrogant Maoist cadres shattered the dignities of democracy, once again, by abusing and restricting citizens who wanted to pass by and mishandled journalists who had come to cover the news of the summit talks. Such profanity for fundamental rights is fast turning them against the democratic value system that has not been necessarily wrapped in the red star worn on their foreheads. Here they wanted to demonstrate that they are powerful without being in power. But without power, history reminds us that there is no communism.

The Kathmandu Post – October 30, 2006

33

Burning Terai

December 25, 2006 Monday was a nightmare for Nepalgunj. The blasted apathy of security officials and administration that encouraged the perpetrators to turn the fateful day an easy art work of terror. The faceless perpetrators doomed the city to hell with one dead, several injured, and properties damaged.

Above all, it has carved a non-evanescent chink in the communal harmony of our society. It was the price Nepalgunj, in particular and the country at large, has paid for the lasciviousness of the Nepal Sadbhavana Party-A (NSP-A) for its parochial view of self declared messiah of the Madhesi.

Then we saw a *tableau vivant*; blame game, resolutions and resolutions, appeal to maintain communal harmony, call for judiciary inquiry, and compensation to victims and finally the boiling emotion culminating into a goodwill rally where the leaders with a grin on their faces throw promises and consolations of worn-out words, as if the nation would have been doomed otherwise.

In the political front the official response of the NSP-A to the tragedy was awfully veneer, when its central committee issued a statement stating that "some regressive and constituent assembly elements had resorted to vandalism to harm the image of the party". How can the NSP-A, a political party that claims working for the Madhesi interest, seemingly absolve itself from the responsibility of the Nepalgunj tragedy that ensued from the *band*?

The political party, that stirs the society by calling a *band*, if it cannot foresee the reaction it would generate to its political call, how can its leaders be considered as discernible? If that is so; what moral ground do they have to claim as the leaders of the Madhesi? The Nepalgunj tragedy has raised this question.

The present Madhesi movement that has been fulminating demanding proportional representation and federal governance is not ennui but has genuine reasons. But the government's myopic vision is unable to see its seriousness. The NSP-A leaders also hopelessly failed to prove themselves as leaders of the Terai (Madhes), which is inhabited by several other ethnic communities since generations along with the Madhesi in majority. Their present understanding and definition of the Madhesi is not only parochial but contentious also, if one goes by logic and not by indignation.

The self-declared mouthpiece of the Terai, the NSP-A and several other outfits of the Terai that claim as wannabe do-gooders of Madhesi rights have wronged the Pahadi people(?) recently matching to xenophobia, thus insinuating the Terai as a Madhesi bastion. It seems that the Madhesi leaders failed to read the writings that the Nepalgunj incidence has left on the wall. You are pushing to create a beachhead of the Pahadi community in the Terai, a moment which will be unfortunate in the history of communal harmony of this country.

In the words of Prime Minister, Koirala, the Nepalgunj incidence is an eye-opener to us. Yes it is, and particularly to the

NSP-A and other political parties that fan the Madhesi-Pahadi sentiment for their political existence, it gives a message that simply because it has been exploited by the ruling elites for decades do not *espo-facto* only take the Terai as guaranteed.

No doubt, the discrimination meted to the Terai in the past is regrettable, but this alone is not the reason that has kept the Madhesi out of the mainstream. One of the important reasons that is responsible for the predicament is their orthodox community with feudal practices which is slow to respond to the changes of time mainly due to lower level of educational awareness. The Madhesi leaders and elites need to do soul-searching with all sincerity and dare to accept their lapse and stop playing blame game only.

There goes again the replay of Nepalgunj picture show at Lahan. A human life is wasted, several injured followed by depredation. This time the political prima-donna was in the guise of apolitical name, the Madhesi People's Rights Forum (MPRF). The MPRF leaders who peddled repetition as reinvention had presented the kitsch of denying rights to the Terai as suppression towards the Madhesi community.

Apparently, what they say seems correct, but if one delves into the issue with all fairness, it is not difficult to find that the Madhesi leaders are politicking their decades of isolation as stake to get power which otherwise is difficult for them through democratic way. These leaders are following the beaten path of the pugnacious Maoists by which they could grab eighty three seats in the interim legislature, without fighting any elections, and nobody knows which constituency they represent to in the house.

In retrospect, the Madhesi leaders who have had represented their community from the time of Bhadrakali Misra to Mahant Thakur and Bedanand Jha to Badri Mandal, we hardly find any of these leaders worth their Madhesi sentiment would ever moot the Terai issue.

The state has made heavy investment in infrastructural development in the Terai as compared to the hills. Consequently, the Terai has developed in these years, but the Madhesi community remained stagnant. Why? It is obvious that the Madhesi leaders and the elites are equally part of the nexus either for their personnel political gain or they were incapable of instilling development in their own society.

The level of awareness in this community is strikingly low, as compared to their Pahadi counterpart who resides side-by-side with them in the Terai, due to lack of education. After the advent of democracy, in 1951 till today, the Madhesi leaders and intellectuals have hopelessly failed to bring social awareness and change in their community commensurate to the need of the time.

Is the incidence of Nepalgunj and Lahan a metaphor of burning Terai? If it is so; why it is burning? The backwash the nation has faced, that has no precedents, suggests that it is more an exercise of demographic arrogance with an apparent underlying political agenda and less a conscientious work of the Madhesi cause. If we put the pieces of jig-saw in their places, a serious picture pops up giving dangerous indications. The way Nepalgunj incidence flared up suggests that it was a handy work of some faceless progressive forces putting the regressive face in front, while Lahan case has vestige of support from outside the country as well. However, these indications need to be substantiated with facts. If it happens to be true, a bigger danger is looming ahead.

Under the prevailing situation, be it the NSP-A, be it the MPRF, or any other outfit, their move could be construed nothing but as an attempt to reach out to the Madhesi vote bank, which has cold-shouldered these leaders in the past in favor of other Madhesi and non-Madhesi leaders who are also equally concerned with the Terai issue but sans communal tint.

The sad part of the incidence is that the Madhesi intellectuals are also fanning the internecine campaign of communal nature hoping to get a piece of pie in case the Madhesi representation swells up. But these so-called elites do not have their constituency and their public support extends not beyond the gallery of their parties.

In these years education level in the Madhesi community has certainly gone up and so also awareness level. The ethos of this conservative community is undergoing a sea change, the throes of which one can feel in the movement. They are floundering for their identity in the national mainstream. They must get their proper share through inclusion.

Definitely, the Terai issue mooted by the Madhesi leaders needs sagacity to address it, as it has all the elements to go astray as the Sri Lankan or Bosnian crisis. Before it engulfs the nation with communal fire, let us hope that it will be doused by the water of wisdom and rationale.

The Kathmandu Post – Febuary 1, 2007

34

CA Poll: To Be or Not To Be

The Maoist law maker Lokendra Bista's bravado for speaking out his mind about the interim parliament and it's respected (?) MPs were an apocalypse of truth. The supercilious demeanor of Bista in the House is the Maoists' propensity to show they are superior and different from others and above the law of the land; that they abhor the bourgeois parliament and give a damn to democracy and they are not afraid to take any one any where. This has evoked awe, but certainly not admiration for the Maoists.

When the parliamentary code of conduct got atomized by the profanity of hubris and impunity, the all-powerful parliament could remain as a looker-on and do nothing but admonition. This gave an impression that the Maoists are the bracketed group with the exclusive membership in the House. Is it not an appeasement or else groveling? These exclusive 83 unequals among the 205 equals have hardly been able to prove their power of clerisy in the House that can sway perceptions and change the life of the nation. The Maoists are good wordsmiths and the House is an alluring place for these demagogues, but they are yet to show their ingenuity to make a qualitative difference in the parliament. Instead, they flaunt the ideological repertoire and walk unchallenged as the pinstriped pachyderms.

Albeit, the Maoists, if they are sincere, are in the throes of democratization process and such situation demands sangfroid in their attitude which is overwhelmingly seen nowhere with these revolutionaries-turned-democrats. The most poignant case is that their supreme leader signs the Comprehensive Peace Agreements (CPA) with the SPA and the government but the cadres in the districts act of their own volition. People could not yet feel that the clauses of the agreements are the binding and guiding principles for the rebels too. They are still ranting as a parallel government in the districts and acting as if they are above the law of the land. The recent deforestation activities, punishing people on their own without any legal code of conduct and taking a pique against anybody anywhere make people feel that they are Neanderthals.

The most worrying part is that such malfeasances are continuing right under the nose of their leaders. The leadership has always ready-made excuses to defend their cadres and absolve them from the blame of their misdemeanor by indulging in public apology and the histrionics of self-criticism. The recent one in the series of melodrama was the apology by the chief whip of the CPN Maoist in the parliament for the string of invectives spewed out by the Maoist lawmaker Bista. If recidivism is their conduct, public apology and self-criticism will be regarded as cruel jokes by the people at large.

Given the Maoists' dimension of culture of impunity and defiance of the government statutes, that the election for the CA will be held in a free and fair environment has a few takers. People were of the opinion that once the rebels enter the parliament they will turn into responsible representatives of people and begin to follow the democratic principles.

But to their utter dismay, the Maoists are still enamoured of terrorizing people by their vitriol, intimidation and brandishing gun in public places. Their obsession with gun shows that they don't believe in the political changes that are happening in the country and are using them either for their strategic purpose or they have some hidden agenda of their own. If it is so, in either case people are beguiled for believing them joining the democratization process.

Under such situation how will people believe the words of the Maoist leaders when they say that free and fair CA election to be held in mid-June? If they are sincere about holding the CA election, their mere words will not convince people rather they have to substantiate it with their deeds as well. First of all, they have to stop behaving as wimps and self-accredited do-gooder to take law into their hands. They should refrain from intimidating people for any purpose wielding their might and accept to play on level field.

Although, the Maoists are at the door-step of joining the interim government, people at large are not yet convinced that this will help hold free and fair CA election, in view of the wide gap between their words and deeds. Among other reasons, the controversy that has cropped up regarding the number of weapons registered with the UNMIN and Prachanda's various statements associated with it made people askance at Maoist's intention of peaceful and fair CA election. Further, in Butwal he said that large numbers of technical cadre who are not registered are living out of the UN monitored cantonments and they are capable of way-laying at several places at a time. This has evoked a serious doubt about the sincerity of the Maoists for holding free and fair CA elections.

Moreover, when he said that their weapons are swept away by river and gutted in fire, people took it as his prank. Serious matter should be said seriously and not in jest. To add salt to the injury, one of the Maoist doyens vaunted in foreign TV that if the government captures two polling booths they would take four during the CA election. Such uncanny statements are enough to act as a cold douche to any one who is rational.

The Maoists should not take people for a ride as they know what is wrong and what is right. Instead of being on the stump, they should rather prove their sincerity and have courage to come forward and declare that they will not join the interim government now and help the government by any means to hold free and fair CA election. Is it too much to expect from the Maoists at this time?

As the Maoist stand on the CA election is veering between poll and post, this gives an impression that they are looking for a plausible excuse if it could be delayed. What is the reason for their volte-face when the CA election is tapping the door?

Before the Madhesi movement snow-balled, Prachanda failed to adapt to the circumstances quickly and read the crowd. He even denied to talk with the leaders of the Madhesi movement and passed derogatory remarks for them. He also suggested the government to move the military along with their Peoples' army to quell the unrest. Madhesis are visibly chafed at the swash-buckling. This has caused a severe loss of the Maoist influence in the Terai and there are indications that the verdict may go against them in the CA election. If the CA election is postponed the happiest person would be the Maoists. No doubt, the king also will have his own reason to be happy. But then is it not an injustice to the mandate of second *Janaandolan*? And will anyone tell who its tutelage authority is?

The Kathmandu Post – March 19, 2007

35

An Idea that Failed

What should one expect from a renegade like Upendra Yadav who is a Maoist-turned self-declared *messiah* of the Madhesi movement and leading the Forum? That he would have clarity of thought, that he would have analytically sharp and precise conclusions which other leaders of Terai could not produce, that he would instill some new insights to bring a qualitative difference in the movement. He is a leader by accident, and was a non-descript before, who belied all such customary intellectual expectations by orchestrating the gory carnage of Gaur. He simply has recycled what he learned from the rabid demagogues – reprisal and rabble-rousing – making the movement riddled with communal fallacies and acute intellectual schizophrenia. Today the Forum as well as the Morcha has become the by-word for a reproach to the Madhesis, in general, because of the infantilism of its so-called leaders. A genuine cause of the Terai (in a limited sense Madhes) has been defeated due to the parochialism of the Madhesi leaders of the movement as well as political parties.

When the Madhesi movement was started the Forum vaunted being a socio-political and economical equalizer, but ended up being an internal destabilizer by disturbing the communal harmony in the country. It has been infiltrated by vested groups of the country and outside to meet their political ends. The Gaur macabre is the glaring example of the perpetrators incognito who are hell-bent to exploit the predicament to the hilt by letting loose the vindictive politics so that the CA poll in waiting could be destabilized.

By almost any measure, the incidence of Gaur deserves condemnation. It was not only unnecessary but a tragic blunder of both the parties involved in it. Both the Forum and the Maoists looked like inebriated pachyderms that know only brute forces and would not play by rules for the sake of their cocky nose. The government is equally blameworthy for the mayhem failing to control it because of its dereliction. Further, its reluctance to go for investigation about the heavy losses of lives and properties during the entire movement purports denigration of the Madhesi movement. This has once again showed the dominance of hill elites in the country's politics and the administration.

While playing in the hands of perpetrators the Forum leaders have squandered many opportunities that could have been proved milestones in resolving the Madhesi issue once for all. But the leaders remained busy in building up their persona as tough guy through spilling communal hatred condescend them to rejectionists. They are good at saying what they do not like, but they do not have any positive thoughts. When the government invited them for dialogue by acquiescing most of their demands, they rejected it forwarding conditions one after another. This shows that they are interested in keeping the communal pot boiling, rather than resolving the issue, by rejecting the dialogue. The fraternal organizations of the Forum, after they knew the reality, denounced its flippancy and dissociated from it. This should be an eye-opener to the Forum leaders that while championing for the cause of the Madhesi community, the communal divide and the secessionist politics, which are run through remote control, are not accepted.

After Gaur incident, the leaders of the Forum had gone in the hideout. If they were right, why did they hide? Today, the Madhesi movement is losing its heat due to the indiscernible acts of the Forum. Almost unnoticed, Upendra Yadav has become ex-poodle in a short stint, because he was an accidental leader pampered by some vested interest and run by remote control. But, by no means, the issue of the identity and inclusion of the Madhesi raised by the movement is of less importance.

While fighting for the inclusion, the Madhesis, certainly, need to do some looking back and soul-searching also. Had the Madhesi leaders, since the advent of democracy in the country, ever made any sincere effort to address this festering issue of discrimination in spite of their regular participation in power, be it in the democratic or the Panchyat era? The annals of history reveals that there is no such effort ever been done by any Madhesi leader at any point of time. Rather, majority of the Madhesi elites always wanted to remain cozy and at times vied among themselves to be at the proximity of power centres of hill elites. If it is so, are not the Madhesis themselves equally responsible for their present predicament? Under such circumstances, the argument of the Madhesi intellectuals resting blame on the 238 years of rule of the hill elites only for their isolation will have very few takers and their argument is regarded as nothing but babble.

The other side of the story, there are scores of non-Madhesi leaders of hill and native origins who are born in the Terai, living in the Terai and had has been working for the Terai cause including the Madhesi one. Their relentless effort has brought the region to the present state of development. Hitherto, they dreamt for the Terai and they lived for the Terai. But the bigoted cadre of the Madhesi movement did not spare the houses and statues of such leaders either. No word of regret or apology for such flippant behavior of the Madhesi activists be they from the Forum, the Morcha or the political parties, is heard. It suggests that Madhesi leaders, *albeit*, live in the 21st century but regrettably with a brain of Neanderthal.

The Madhesi movement would have been a magnum opus, had it been a terai movement rather than a Madhesi only. The protagonists of the movement and their protégé are all seemingly obsessed with the Indian mind due to geographical and cultural intimacy. There is no harm in appreciating Indian goodness. But the paradox is, for them the Indians who came and settled here only two or three decades ago and obtained the citizenship are genuine Madhesis whereas people of hill and native origins who are born here and living for generations are aliens. This is a dangerous outlook that inculcates pathology of distrust in the Madhesi mindset.

The earlier tempo of the Madhesi movement has lost its heat as it failed to encompass all sons of the Terai soil. Because of the communal hue of the movement several Terai natives publicly announced that they do not like to be called or included as the Madhesis. And this has proved a leviathan setback to the movement. The sectarian mindset of the Madhesi movement has defeated its bigger cause and is the *raison d'être* for its trivialization. Upendra Yadav, Goit, Singh and their brigand who hold on to the trigger from the black hole are yet to realize the reality. Earlier they realize it lesser the country bleeds.

The Kathmandu Post – April 16, 2007

36

Bhutan: A Lost Shangri-La

If history does not repeat itself, it certainly comes back to haunt us. Bhutan's new King Jigme Khesar and his government are witness to that. They are caught in ideological morass of "one nation, one language," which is an outlandish shibboleth of the past, where the society is a mosaic of diversity of religion, culture and language. King Jigme Singye was trying to render the country in a monotonous sectarian monolith. He had driven out a majority of the southern population called Lhotshampas, who are people of Nepali origin, from the country, to the extent of ethnic cleansing. He was hell bent to prove that the Lhotshampas as unbecoming citizens of Bhutan. This is the legacy the new king has inherited willingly or unwillingly. Therefore, in Bhutan and outside, depending on who is writing, the King Wangchuck is painted as black and white for his policies adopted on national security, citizenship, education, culture, dress code, etc.

The untold *raison d'être* for his policy is his perceived threat of the Lhotshampa's growing influence on Bhutanese way of life and its body politique. In spite of the King Wangchuck's spectre, the other citizens are a permanent member of the Bhutanese scruples, which he failed to expunge it from their psyche. He, therefore, in the pretext of national integration and unity let down the Lhotshampas by pursuing the politics of paranoia dressed up by the *Ta wa sum* (king, country, people) and other draconian measures that every autocratic ruler promulgates in one form or other forgetting the lessons from history. The recent events of Nepal should have been an eye opener to Bhutan and its monarchy, but much to the chagrin of international community, the king seems opinionated about its policy towards the Lhotshampas and his political dissidents.

But for Bhutan watchers, the country is struggling with itself to justify the King Wangchuck's ethnic cleansing, where the Lhotshampas' every past act of nation-building is looked as infidelity now, and they are branded as Ngolop (anti-national/rebel). The high drama enacted in the National Assembly of Bhutan in many occasions and the so-called public consultation meetings held in every district during the preparation of the 7th Five-Year-Plan in 1992 were a few examples of the orchestrated move of the hardliners to goad the king for apartheid law against the Lhotshampas in the name of threat to national security and cultural identity of Bhutan.

In the era of new world order, where democracy, human rights, pluralism, etc. are the practice of the day, Bhutan is still dwelling in medieval mindset and run by an autocrat in the name of the Dharmaraja single-handedly. Here, key persons and policy makers, including the ministers are appointed by the king, yet. Freedom of speech is non-existent and media is a government mouth piece. Recently, there was a cosmetic display of freedom of speech by promoting two private newspapers, but were guided by the government. This is a country where there are no opposition and human rights organizations who could speak for people, and, yet Bhutan government claims that it practices democracy.

By disfranchising one fifth of its total population from citizenship right it is shamelessly claiming that it is going to hold a democratic election in the year 2008. The King Jigme Khesar, who is educated in England, must be wondering at as what kind of democracy his apparatchiks are talking about? In fact, the advocacy of democracy by the feudal servitors is a ploy to strengthen royal absolutism so that the political dissidence could be smothered up further. We have seen and lived that sort of democracy in Nepal during the Panchayat regime. The recent abdication of the Golden throne by the King Jigme Singye in favor of his eldest son could be seen in this perspective and very likely it is a process patching up his family feud, because of which the arcane monarchy is fast losing its traditional constituency.

The King Jigme Singye can go on rhapsodizing democratic transition in Bhutan in his soliloquies to hoodwink international communities, but his actions that made his own nationals refugees and languishing in the camps prove that he cannot be regarded as a reformist. The most shameful part is that for sixteen years the king had been lying that the refugees are non-Bhutanese, but after long dilly-dallying by Bhutan, when a joint-verification was carried out in one of the seven camps at the Khudunabari, from more than 12,000 refugees of that camp, 80 percent or so were found to be Bhutanese who have some sorts of documents to prove it.

Upon finding this result, the royal government of Bhutan impudently stopped the bilateral talks on repatriation since 2003, in the pretext of a preempted scuffle between the refugees and the Bhutanese officials at the camp. Under the given situations when the king talks about holding democratic election, India, the United States and the European governments eerily remain mute, this encourages the despot to justify his undemocratic action of ethnic cleansing in the cover of democracy.

World community should not forget the lesson from history that if the refugee crisis is neglected for long, the indignation can breed anything like Palestinian crisis which has endangered the Middle East and the world at large. Looking at the geographical location of Bhutan, its proximity to the vulnerable region of the Chicken neck and the presence of scores of insurgent out-fits in the Northeast India extending to Bangladesh and Myanmar, the Bhutanese refugee crisis should not be left unattended by India to fester.

Particularly, the visible success of the Maoists in Nepal once it settles here, it can go to any length because of their dogmatism and fraternization guts. Let the Last Shangri-La not be the Lost Shangri-La.

India, which should have indulged in solving the crisis, is keeping itself at bay branding it as the bilateral concern of Nepal and Bhutan. But everybody knows that India cannot brush its hands off from this issue as it is both ways, directly and indirectly, involved in making of the refugees. This is not the political era of either Rajiv Gandhi in India or King Birendra in Nepal. If the Congress, in Delhi, can sit in coalition government with the DMK party of Tamilnadu which once supported the LTTE of Sri Lanka, why Delhi and Kathmandu can not find a common ground, without compromising their national interests, on the Bhutanese refugee issue?

Without wasting much time India should start studying the refugees' psyche, rather than viewing the situation through the unfocussed binocular of the King Jigme's wishful thinking.

The Kathmandu Post – May 22, 2007

37

Robin Hood Culture

A little nudge, perhaps, meant to create a ripple only has been producing a gigantic wave in the country's political scenario. Pushpa Kamal Dahal alias Prachanda, the Maoist chairman, recently in an interview on the CNN-IBN television said that he wants to be the president of Nepal in two years' time, does not know whether he is waving or drowning. But one thing is obvious that the sound-bite has been heard loud and clear by the politicos in the country. Minister of Peace and Reconstruction, Ram Chandra Paudel remained *blasé* about the statement and has ruled him out becoming the president of the country branding him as an authoritarian. We do not know if the minister Paudel is a sooth-sayer, but for Prachanda, the going may get tougher if he really meant what he said in the TV interview, particularly in the light of the strategic design to capture the state power by turning the country as a Ruritanian state through anomie by its front-line outfits like the Young Communist League (YCL).

A brazen dialectic demagogue, traveling through several compromises in the guise of 12-point, 8-point agreements and so on, no doubt, he finds himself at the centre stage of the national politics, only to challenge his rigmarole on the ideology he adhered to so dearly, in the quest of emerging as a winner in a draw situation that has ensued the understanding he forged with the Seven-Party Alliance (SPA).

Albeit, it is early to predict on Prachanda's dream, if it comes true, but one can recall bigger burlesques that the country has witnessed in the past. Remember the transit Prime ministers Man Mohan Adhikari and Sher Bahadur Deuba and the accidental ruler the King Gyanendra have born out of situations when the disagreement was the mother of confusion. They did not have the mandate of the nation; rather their fleeting rule was a divorce from the ideological philosophy for the realization of a private fantasy and ego on the national account.

What Prachand has uttered about his wish, if it translates into more than platitudes, remains to be seen. Joining the SPA government three months ago, the saga of their running the government eloquently speaks the duplicity of the Maoists. They are in the government enjoying all the facilities that are paid by public taxes, but they continue spewing sharp anti-establishment rhetoric behaving as if they are in the opposition. The row between the Minister for Forest and Soil Conservation Matrika Yadav and the Prime Minister, the handling of the Melamchi with the Asian Development Bank by the Minister for Works and Physical Planning Hisila Yami and the Maoist law maker Lokendra Bista's cocky behaviour in the parliament were a few examples of utter disgrace to the cabinet system and the parliament of democratic polity.

Further, to add insult to the injury, the devious way of planting the YCL cadres in the ministries, to get people's work done through them reminds the hay days of the Panchyat era, is the talk of the town among the government service receivers. Is this kind of governance Pranchanda is looking for to provide Nepalis people, if his party commands majority in the parliament? The Maoist's vaudeville of salvation politics has a very few takers now. People see the street savvy YCL manhandles the government's representative (CDO) in the office in the district and its mother party, who is the coalition partner in the government, does not feel necessary to speak a single word of repent let alone the condemnation. The corporate houses, business establishments and private people are requested (?) for extortion unabatedly yet. We have newspapers with news of intimidation and corporal threat once they are opposed and criticized as if they are above rest of other Nepalis and beyond censor. People are beholding their rant of self-righteousness around but the Maoist leaders, the YCL and their ministers trim with tinsel. Do not take people for a ride for they can differentiate the rhetoric from their track record.

Politics has become a Machiavellian phenomenon and, for the sake of political gains, even evils are regarded as worth patronizing and rapscallions, if they are strategically placed, are worth coddling. The revelation by the Maoist top brass about their relationship with the Palace excoriates its double face. The same moral warrior has once said that if the government agrees with constituent assembly the Maoists are ready to accept the monarchy also. Does there any line exist that separates their ideology from the strategy? Both these forces warmed up each other to fail the multiparty democracy in the past. Had they succeeded, Nepal would have been reeling under the dictatorship of either extreme right or left today. To cover up their profligacy, both do not hesitate to reiterate impudently that what they do is for the good of common people. Today the same once-the-bedfellows are vying for one another's neck.

Because of such habit of moral imperium, what kind of government people would expect from these two extreme forces, if either of them happens to be the president or remains as the king of Nepal? Or the same political parties who had failed to deliver but never tried to makeover themselves a sacrosanct. Their misdemeanor, if proved by law is always culpable. Perhaps, once again we may have to settle for the lesser among the evils.

For common people, the government is supposed to be a stabilizing force in the society. Its mandate is to raise the living standard of people by providing equal opportunities through judicious distribution of resources. The less privileged are given special attention. This is the theory. The Maoists have simply redefined the paradigm into modern version of the Robin Hood economics. During the period of their people's war the Maoists have looted several banks and private properties, extorted and intimidated whom they deem necessary with their self-righteous imperium. Extortion and intimidation are still in practice even after joining the government.

Of course, one needs huge resources to launch people's war for such a long period and the Maoists have collected that resources through various illegal means. As the war has now ended and the Maoists are in the government as well, as a responsible party they should feel obliged to give an account of the booty to the public, so that, common people can feel that the said people's war was fought for them. If the Maoists fail to do this, there would be little difference between them and the then royal regime which has also misappropriated huge amount of state's resources in the name of quelling the democratic revolution – *Janandolan II* and did not produce any account of its expenditure.

The Maoists should realize that the practice of Robin Hood culture can not justify their version of secularism. It is equity in policy and practice that in true sense delivers democracy. Otherwise, Robin Hood, despite the nimbus, whatever said and done, was a highway brigand.

The Kathmandu Post – July 13, 2007

38

Spooky Pre-conditions

Major political parties of the interim parliament and outside when acquiesced to hold it, so, who is afraid of the Constituent Assembly (CA) poll to happen on November 22? Let us not be an irrational believer that the question of CA election has been settled for good because the government of the Eight-Party Alliance (EPA) announced its date indulging an extensive consultation with its alliance partners. If it is so, why did Prachanda, the chairman of the CPN-M, need to set two pre-conditions: declaration of a republic and a fully-proportional representation system for the CA poll, prior to the CA election? The major political parties and leaders of civil societies have not only rejected it but also blamed the Maoists of trying to stymie the historic CA poll by raising the issues that had been already agreed earlier.

The Maoists may put forward their own theorem in favor of Prachanda's pre-conditions, as they are regarded as good wordsmiths, but for general public it is like *en-fant terrible.* They wonder what the credibility of the commitments the Maoists make is, if they reject it when it is not favourable to them. It seems that the spectre of Lenin's criticism of left wing infantilism of communist movement still haunts them as a ghost story.

Why did Prachanda do it? And that too, why after the political agreement of November 8, till the other day when he was panegyrizing CA poll as a panacea for the country? The most obvious explanation, of course, could be that the CPN-M has been on a downhill slide since it joined the coalition government four months ago and its young league's social-service-development-terror aggrandized it. It also failed to read the zeitgeist correctly and thus it has lost the Terai from its influence now. Prachanda's bullying remark to mobilize the Nepal Army and the Maoist Army to tackle the Terai crisis was not only irresponsible one but it proved unproductive as well for which the CPN-M had to pay its price through the Gaur carnage. The incidence was terrible and deplorable by everyone, but there was a mute public opinion floating around like it was a lesson the Maoists had to learn about how they need to respect others. However, ensuing the Maoists-related events suggest that they are not a good learner.

Joining the bandwagon of Seven Party Alliance (SPA), the CPN-M has kept the party line divided, which was prominently visible in the extended meeting of the fifth plenum of the CPN-M, a party where dissent is intolerable and submission to the politburo diktats has no alternative. Against all communist protocol, Prachanda, the powerful chairman of the CPN-M has come under the severe criticism of hardliners. The setting of the two pre-conditions on the CA poll at this stage is nothing but the testimony of acquiescence of their censure by the party chairman.

A party which believes in perpetual fighting needs to invent always new enemy to fight with and these pre-conditions of the Maoists will definitely invent them enough enemies to fight to their satisfaction, only condition is how bad the country will bleed remains as a matter of guess.

In the reflected glow of renunciation and peaceful mainstreaming the CPN-M could not shine as anticipated by the backroom dialecticians. Rather, they are now confronted with a stark truth that they would not perform very well in the coming CA poll, particularly in the Terai. In this context the setting of pre-conditions is fraught with intrigue to eschew the poll, no matter, what has befallen the country. The comrades have a tendency to excel in incongruities because they have nothing at stake to lose except a few scrounged slogans and a fossilized ideology of Marx, Lenin and Mao, since, they already have lost Nepal when they fought a self-declared people's proxy war with the help of the RIM and the COMPOSA like outfits which don't have any stake here neither for the country nor for the welfare of Nepalis.

Maoists' perception of the CA poll is deeply ambivalent but they perceive it as a character to emulate. Divided mind, double standard and glib tongue of their leaders have earned the CPN-M a name – a party of convenience. So long as such mannerism remains dominant in the Maoist psyche, there will be a few takers of the Maoist whooper. People do not find match between their words and deeds.

The Maoists want power; they want to be the ruler of the country as their chairman Prachanda gave vent to his wish that he would like to be the president of the country in two years time. But the comrades knew that it is not possible as Nepal is neither North Korea nor Afghanistan of the late seventies. Therefore, they took a devious route to get power by joining the SPA government. Because of their swaggering persona they believed that they can create a situation where the "tail will wag the dog." But in a short period of four months they realized that all along it indeed the dog that was wagging the tail. This was, of course, a very painful apocalypse for the comrades and hence, there is a big hullabaloo in the party line especially among hardliners to withdraw from the government.

The noise was conspicuously heard in the Balaju Plenum meeting also. The party leadership giving a patient hearing to all dissenting voices, as anticipated, decided to remain in the government and continue working with the major political parties whom the Plenum categorically branded as bourgeois. Hello, comrades! Can ideology be traded for power?

While the apparatchiks are busy inventing king and his regression as a bogyman for the CA poll, some recent opinion polls suggest that the CPN-M would not fare above 10-15 percent of voting. Class and caste, in spite of all modernity, had always made its presence felt during the elections in the past. In the quest of crafting a classless and casteless society, on its flip-side, the CPN-M has created a divide in the ethnic mosaic of the country, thus caste and class will continue to remain as a biggest incomprehension of the Maoist party.

The Kathmandu Post – August 13, 2007

39

Maoists in Rejection

As the Constituent Assembly (CA) poll is zeroing in, the CPN (Maoist) is dithering lest people's verdict and playing gimmicks – the latest one in the row is their mentioning of revival of the iniquitous kangaroo court and pulling out of the government. If it happens, it would be the most unfortunate event that might further delay the republic making of the country.

The Maoists' *faux pas* insinuates that common people do not have a crush on it, if there is no intimidation, because of the atrocities they have perpetrated during their self-declared people's proxy war. It was a time when this party was regarded as a terrorist group by the state and lived in arguments. It was a storehouse of fossilized ideology and an artifact of the Maoist dogma that remained literally incompatible with other political parties which believed in democracy, plurality and free market.

The political dynamics established by the 1990 revolution was atomized when the dynastic ego of King Gyanendra wanted to rule the roost. It suddenly created a space for the

Maoists to join hands with the political parties that were fighting against the king's regression. That brought about a history-shifting, the 12-point compact changing the political power structure. This must have taken King Gyanendra by surprise, as at one point of time the Maoists and he was coaxing each other to destabilize democracy – a fact that has remained no more a secret now.

That was then. The CPN (Maoist) is a political force now. It is no more regarded as a terrorist brigand and is a responsible partner in the coalition government. They showed their bargaining skill by tugging eighty three of their cadres as legislatures in the Interim Parliament. As members of the parliament they are people's representatives, but weirdly their constituencies do not extend beyond the TV cameras, seminars and press briefings. *Albeit*, they are a major partner in the government, they are pitting against it as an opposition – a parody on democracy. This is a cliché-ridden strategy of propaganda of communist culture to keep inventing new enemies so that their cadres can remain occupied and not allowed to think otherwise.

Neither in the government nor in the Interim Parliament the performance balance sheet of the CPN (Maoist) is something the common people can be proud of. The fanatic barons fail to reflect the national zeitgeist. There is a conspicuous absence of power of clerisy in the party that could sway the perception with the power of ideas.

In the Interim Parliament they proved to be a huge let-down as its legislatures could not go beyond the beaten path of populist-propaganda attitude that could transform the party into a new and contemporary one. They scored miserably low in political morality and democratic decencies. Their image is least of lawmakers and more of law breakers who are not equal among the equals whose demeanour are above the country's law.

Revolutionaries are effective agitators who can stir and sway people's sentiment but they do not necessarily need to be good statesmen as well. When the Maoist leadership accepted that their ministers in the cabinet and legislatures in the parliament could not perform effectively, if this is his earnest revelation, the Maoists must have realized now that running statecraft needs a different skill than fighting a war.

This failure of the Maoists is bound to affect their performance in the coming CA poll. Realizing this situation the hardliners in the party are hell bent on postponing the CA poll and pressing hard Prachanda to pull out from the government. The 22-point demand and the round table meeting could be taken as a harbinger of it. It is also an indication that hawks are in domination in the party after the Balaju plenum. Under such situation it is interesting to watch how comrade Prachanda would influence the transformation and mainstreaming of his party which is an untold prerequisite for international acceptance.

A party that should be ideally in the junkyard of the history is alliteratively trying to change the agenda that has already been set by the Interim Parliament as mandated by the April revolution: election of the CA and restructuring of the state. Their various explanations to defer the CA poll sound much like glib talk; their shifting official voices resonate like poly-pranks. If one listens to the incongruous statements of their leaders about the tapping CA poll that overwhelmingly suggests nothing but their make-believe to delay it, despite their claim that the CA election is their agenda which Prachanda had once projected it as a bargaining chip in favor of the monarchy.

Government's determination to hold the CA poll on 22 November has lodged the CPN-M in the dock. Despite being the signatory of the decision, the leaders of this party are hounded by the bogey of the palace, reactionary and foreign forces and do not lose time to draw a red-herring as their two pre-conditions to hold the CA poll in the stipulated time. All the Maoist rank and file is harping on it as true followers of Joseph Goebbels, but except rhetoric one does not find any substance in it. Thus they have failed to convince people effectively and come out with a credible counterpoint.

After the qualitative shift of the CPN (Maoist) by joining the mainstream, it seems that its untold strategy is to grab power without going for people's verdict. Prachanda's backtrack on the CA poll can be viewed as an effort to arrogate to himself to a position of supremacy which is a communist culture very much akin to Castro in Cuba, Kim in North Korea and leaders in China. For communists, after all, the masses are nothing but amorphous abstraction to acquiesce.

If the CA poll happens, how the CPN (Maoist) takes part in it is everybody's enquiry. What we see is this party has lost its distinctiveness as a party of law abiding common people. In the Terai it is almost becoming a non entity. In other parts of the country it is still riding piggyback of terror and intimidation. Ideologically in delusion and with no fresh and new ideas, the party has failed to catch up with times and lost its rhetorical edge as well.

Let us not rear a folly that the CPN (Maoist) is a party that stands against the bourgeois system. Rather, we see it is a coalition partner in the government with the Nepali Congress, which its politburo has identified as a bourgeois party. The witlessness of the left party can be seen anywhere anytime, when Madhav Nepal once declared that the regression was half corrected and joined the then government. Today the same party is frisking on the CA poll announcement.

The Kathmandu Post – September 17, 2007

40

The Undertaker

The ghosts of the past seldom get exorcized and people believe that they undoubtedly return to haunt the future. The Prime Minister Girija Prasad Koirala could barely afford to ignore that truism when he took the audacious gamble sixteen months ago on bringing the CPN (Maoist) into the mainstream politics by signing the 12-point and later the 8-point agreements and Comprehensive Peace Accord with them.

This has, of course, given a new dimension to the national body politics where the Maoists gained enough turf which they were not able to capture through the might of their guns while fighting even for a decade. But looking at the Maoist psyche after the extended plenum of Balaju one feels that either they are into a rut or they have lost the ability to appreciate what is good for them and what would have been better for the nation. They have not yet desisted from looking everything through their dogmatic binocular and their makeover thus is doubtful.

The Maoists joined the government with the SPA and while in the government they had avowed to hold the CA polls thus using every opportunity for their political advantage.

But when they were in the power for a little over five months they had seen more controversies than trophies because of their intransigent persona and cocky ego. In spite of their harangues they are found interested only with their political gains and safe landing of their cadres and the PLA showing apathy towards the problem a common man faced in his daily life. This has pushed their popularity downhill that has landed them in a catch 22 situation where they are no longer ready to face the CA polls.

Putting two preconditions before the CA polls the Maoists wanted to salvage their declining image, but such vaudeville of salvation politics has shattered their credibility further. Had they accepted to go for the CA polls as agreed, people would have hailed them as a savior and deliverer, but blinded by the reverie of becoming an absolute power wielder the Maoists deserted their own pledge thus rendering Prachanda more as a spoiler than a redeemer today. He has baulked people of their chance to become sovereign and be governed by them.

Albeit, the interim parliament has passed the negotiated proposals of the CPN (Maoist) and the UML by a simple voice vote and if it is implemented as such by the government it is an overstepping of constitutional domain that will draw a constitutional crisis. The Maoists are well aware of the fact but yet pushing the government to implement the proposals, it is not because of any new-found bonhomie. It is a desperate move of the Maoists to push the CA polls at bay and to gain the losing ground in the Terai politics trying to establish themselves as a strident espousal of the Terai interests. But this calisthenics, instead of their face-lifting, has debunked their ambivalent perception.

Joining the government as carousel, the Maoist ministers, law makers and their leaderships then realized that it was easier said than done. But then it was already late to uplift their sliding image and they had no alternative but to withdraw from the government.

Today, the country is reeling under anomie because the Maoists want to have their finger in every pie thus seemingly the Maoist spook is desperate to come out of the sarcophagus. To the Maoists' credit today several destabilizing forces are emulating them in the country.

The volt-face of the Maoists on the above two agenda not only contradicts their earlier stand they agreed with the SPA but it gives a buffet to those who believe on their commitments. Not long ago when they were on negotiation table, the Maoist supremo had tried to cajole the then government to swap the CA with the monarchy. Today, the same Maoists are recklessly adamant to and had stymied the CA polls. It is indeed a parody and the country is waiting to behold a bigger burlesque to come.

By definition the political parties in democracy are supposed to be representatives of people and thereby they put tongue to people's wishes and aspirations. That is the theory. Political parties have simply redefined the paradigm into the modern-day version of make use of politics. To be fair, no single party has ever hesitated to practice it but the Maoists have taken it to new levels of sophistry ever since they have joined the open politics. To cover up their profligacy, they always claim that they are doing it to save the nation and not to satisfy any lust for power. But how come they got the moral imperium to talk on behest of people when they are neither elected representatives nor have ever faced people's verdict? They are behaving as if they are the sole arbiter of destiny of the Nepalis.

Playing the same chestnut the Maoists had always treated the royalists as an anathema who would not allow the CA polls to happen. But today the fact is, it is the Maoists who had queered the pitch for the CA polls and not the royalists. What change of heart political savvy Prachand beholds in 'nationalist royalists' that inspired him to call for an alliance with them. His statement is an epitome of real face of the Maoists which suggests that the CPN (Maoist) is not a people centrist party. His apprehensive statement *ipso-facto* insinuates that, first the Maoists' democratic credential is not trustworthy and second autocrats either of left or right are in tandem. Both do not consider people as a source of power, they merely use them.

His statement also reveals their mindset how desperate they are to grab the power for which they can go to anywhere but not to the people. This has turned their glory into dust and at the same time mooted a question – Has the April revolution given mandate to any political party, for this matter the Maoists, to align with the royalists who are anti-republic and has always supported the repressive moves of the kings?

It seems that Prachanda is trying to redefine the mandate of the April revolution on his own volition. This may be much like King Gyanendra's tryst with democracy where he risked discovering the spectre of scepter, but people rejected his foolery. Because of his brinkmanship the monarchy has to look for a place at a necropolis. We hope that the Maoists are not looking for obsequies, like the monarchy did, in the quest of rediscovering the spectre of Mao.

The Kathmandu Post – December 14, 2007

41

A Bee in the Bonnet

The year 2008 has seen a kickoff of a new political party, the Terai-Madhes Loktantrik Party (TMLP), in the country with much media hype by the apostates belonging to different mainstream political parties. Its prima-donna is Mahant Thakur, a Nepali Congress (NC) minister, who later resigned from his position and the party as well. He was a confidant of Prime Minister Girija Prasad Koirala and yet he turned renegade; why? Is it because after four decades of his association with the NC (as quoted by media that needs official vindication) he suddenly realized that the Madhesis are discriminated against by the ruling elites (Pahadi) and living in a state of internal colonization and thus needs a savior? The other leaders of this party on the row, who pose they are larger than the party, are also renegades who had always remained at the helm of power with the ruling elites hand in hand, be it during the Panchayat regime or thereafter.

To these self-declared messiahs why the apocalypse of truth did not come earlier when they were wallowing in power corridor or has someone touted them to realize? Perhaps this is a weird thought, but if this is the truism, the country is waiting for bigger burlesques in future.

Thakur was neither a deliverer nor redeemer ever and he does not have the mystique of the NC with him now but yet he risked bigger than his own size. It is not very difficult to guess that he definitely has blessing of some "invisible hand" that encouraged him to undertake that venture. Can and will Thakur and his party and other Madhesi outfits remain away from communal politics, once autonomy and proportional representation are achieved? This is something political observers are watching!

Although it is tempting to pin the blame for the Terai crisis upon the ruling elites and political leadership, but if one is honest it is an irrefutable fact that unemployment, economic decline and character of the people and its hopelessly antique class and social structure are some of the veritable reasons no less profound for the debasement of the Madhesi people and their underdeveloped predicament. Why do the Madhesi leaders dither to soul-searching when the Pahadi elites have to take their share of blame for untold discrimination made against the Terai and its people?

When one looks at the facade of the TMLP, it portrays no better than the Nepal Sadbhavana Party and other communal outfits, at least in its alliteration, that have spawned in the Terai in recent years. The party has demonstrated that it is *cap-á-pie* anti-Pahadi frisson when Mahant Thakur spewed that the government should remove all the Pahadi staff from its offices in the Terai. His flippant remark clearly demonstrated the flare of demographic arrogance against Pahadi minority in the Terai crossing the line of communal harmony. This insinuates that the TMLP will have no space for the Pahadi community rendering it into a second generation Sadbhavana Party. As things stand now will the TMLP be a party of national status? One has to wait and watch.

Beholding the present trend of the Madhesi politics what should one like me, who is born and brought up in the Terai and living there for generations, expect from the proselytes; that they would have clarity of thought, that they would have analytically precise judgement which others (particularly, Pahadis) could not produce, that they would uncover some new insights of inclusiveness that will enlighten us all. Much to the chagrin, these leaders, who are ranting as if they are the sole arbiter of the Terai destiny, belied all such customary intellectual expectations when they protected and exacerbate the ego of the communal politicians in the name of majority and targeted at the minority to keep the communal pot boiling.

On many occasions the government has reiterated that it can negotiate on any agenda except the authority of self-determination. But the Madhesi leaders are shunning the parley in the make-believe of different conditions. This suggests that they want to keep the pot boiling till they get everything they are demanding. If it is so, you do not need a negotiation or parley but a war to win where you get everything that you are looking for as a winner. If one believes in negotiation it is always a mutual give-and-take phenomenon where neither part wins or loses.

In order to keep the communal pot boiling in the Terai, the country is rife with apprehension that India is playing a role. There may be plausible reasons to believe, but one stark fact we have to accept is that we cannot change the geography and thus India will always have its interest in Nepal and so will have Nepal. What is wrong in it? It is the skill of our leaders that they should be able to manipulate that interest diplomatically into a mutual interest without grovelling at India.

We have a history that whenever Nepal was in need India has helped us. Yet anti-India sentiment is a seminal idea embedded here as a function of communist nationalism and at a time rhetorical nationalism propagated by the Palace to safeguard its own interest – the Kalapani and the Gurkha recruitment issues are a few examples of it. Above all, India's big brotherly attitude to have its finger in every pie in Nepal is also no less responsible for that predicament. Of course bad blood is at both sides too, Bhutanese refugee issue is its example where Nepal is left to face the brunt of ethnic cleansing of the Bhutan's autocratic government with insinuating support of India.

India should look at its next door countries, Pakistan and Afghanistan, where with the US backing Pakistan nurtured the militant groups; Taliban in Afghanistan and armed insurgents as freedom fighters in Kashmir. Pakistan used these militant groups to further its own interest in these countries. But it so happened now that these militant groups have turned into the Frankenstein monster who are not under the control of its mentors, the USA and Pakistan, and are perpetrating havoc on them. Osama bin Laden, now the most hated terrorist by the Americans, is the creation of the US government in the past to serve its interest in Afghanistan against the then Soviet Union.

There are several such examples in the history where creating Frankenstein has always come back on its masters. If India learns from the history, it will definitely not go for such adventure to burn its hand in the Terai, although we hear that the Terai militants are riddled with Indian agents of various hues of criminal and fundamental Hindu extremist outfits. These Frankenstein monsters will definitely grow by the time and evidences show that, on many occasions, they have gone out of control of their mentors once their interest clashed. Will the Nepal-India border remain peaceful then?

These Madhesi leaders taking refuge in the fantasy of one autonomous Terai are basking in the glow of "invisible hand." But if our peaceful border turns into the one like the LOC of

India and Pakistan, where both the countries will need to beef up their security in an unprecedented manner to uphold calm, who will pay the price of it? Of course, the innocent denizens living on both sides of the border.

The Kathmandu Post – January 31, 2008

42

Drool Maoists

A just cause going dangerously wrong: that is holding a free and fair CA poll. The harangues and hyperboles of the Maoist leaders are no near to the popular verdict that distastes their hubris and marauding behaviour which they flaunt as their hallmark. In spite of signing agreement after agreement by their leaders, the YCL is yet going berserk demonstrating the ambivalent perception of the Maoists regarding the free and fair CA poll. This is the same chestnut when the Maoist demagogues, playing to the gallery, whine if they lose in the CA poll, another revolution will ensue. Hello comrade! If that is the bottom line, your frills to the meretricious speeches and manifesto do not make any sense as people can see through your ravenous appetite for power incognito.

To add insult to injury, the criminal brigands in the Terai imbued with communal hatred posturing as political outfits are waylaying on common people, cadres and candidates of the CA poll of political parties and the establishment alike lest decimation of their interest in keeping the communal pot boiling. The Terai is rife with the news that these outfits are hell-bent that the CA poll should not be held.

The inability of Ian Martin and his team of the UN peace keeping mission to tame the Maoists in the cantonments as per the agreements has raised qualm in the minds of common people about the mission's sincerity. The Maoists come out from the camps in combat dress with UN stickered weapons to join their party's poll campaign. The UN mission remains as a mute onlooker simply by issuing a statement against it. Its mission chief declares in media that he simply cannot control them going out from the camps. Is not the mission's conduct tantamount to flirtation with the Maoists? What are they there for? If the CA poll is derailed or hampered due to the Maoists' cause, the UN peace mission cannot remain free from blame.

If the CA poll is to happen under such adverse situation where coercion is undeclared strategy of the Maoists, in spite of their embellished manifesto, the Maoists' New Nepal which they peddle round the country is nothing better than a "Republic of Fear." The Maoists have failed to expunge that fear psychosis from the minds of common people. If there is no such thing up their sleeves they must renounce and fetter the YCL and its intimidating activities, otherwise the YCL unbound is a repudiation of the commitments the Maoist leaders had made through various agreements.

The CA poll is knocking at the door, yet people could not feel secure to cast their vote as the YCL's intimidation is running amok. The Maoists are behaving as if they are both arbiter and executants and its YCL is looking as *enfant terrible* by design. When we look at the concatenation the Maoists are very seriously following a conspiracy theory to explain their possible defeat in the CA poll. The drool is, they see conspiracy only if they are defeated in the poll. Such totalitarian mindset has a long way to go for transformation before they are regarded as civil citizens of pluralistic and free society.

The Maoists, no doubt, when they are on stump, are astute politicians and always play with semantics. But this time people did not appreciate their *bons-mots* and one such example is their conspiracy theory. They have been hawking this theory *ad nauseam* where common people understood it as their signal not to go for a fair play on level-field.

Secondly, Maoists have obstructed and attacked on the poll campaigns of other political parties in various districts under different pretexts. This was not only unfortunate but it was violation of the election Code of Conduct as well. For this matter the other parties are also no saints, but such violations have been recorded more against the Maoists than any other parties. Invariably violence has ensued in all these squabbles where human losses have been reported. The loss of human lives is more in number from the Maoist side than from any other political parties. Loss of human life in a civilized society cannot be accepted in the name of any ideology.

When the Maoists are blamed for the leaders of other political parties being attacked and their poll campaigns obstructed in villages, they curtly argued that it is Nepali people who resented them and the Maoists cadres are not involved in those brawls. While bringing slander against other political parties, the Maoists tend to forget a popular aphorism that is in vogue – do as you would be done by others. Later, when the Maoist leaders and its cadres are also affronted in the similar manner, they failed to notice that Nepali people, if they do not like the Maoist's whopper, can attack on them also like other parties – if the theory remains the same. But the Maoist leadership blames other rival political parties for such action against them and behold conspiracy of regressive forces. Political observers see it as the Maoists do not want to play a fair game based on universal norms and they like to prove that they are more equal among equals and, therefore, cannot be challenged.

There is a reason to repudiate the Maoists not because of their felony and ranting demeanor, but because the ideology they are trying to resurrect is *ante-di-luvian* and irrational in a pluralistic and free society.

Today, Nepalis are talking about a New Nepal of forward looking vision and because of it we are trying to get rid of monarchy which is 238-year-old. But the Maoists are flogging a dead horse of Marxism which is also more than one-hundred-year-old doctrinaire of communism that tries to establish an absolute ruler. Nepalis very little believe that the Maoists who are still in the dogmatic cocoon of the Marxism, an old and failed ideology, will be able to see through the twenty-first century's aspirations unless they come out of it. Therefore, the restructuring of the nation cannot be trusted to the Maoists whose binocular is focused towards one direction only.

The Kathmandu Post – April 8, 2008

43

PM Dahal's China Sojourn

Call it the ghost of his brinkmanship. When Pushpa Kamal Dahal, the chief of CPN (Maoist), thinks his deft political footwork is ready to deliver result, it returns to haunt him. The newly elected Prime Minister Dahal had to undergo such ordeal when he had visited China to attend the closing ceremony of the Beijing Olympics. With his China sojourn India was out of humor and could not remain without demur. It did produce a ripple in the rank and file of the CPN (Maoist) and also attracted censure in the gallery of power centers. Realizing the damage it has inflicted, the comrades started floundering through their rhetoric to normalize it by saying that it was an event specific visit and need not be seen as a bilateral one. But when the Indian and the American envoys did not attend the customary sending-off and receiving ceremony of the prime minister at the airport, it has undoubtedly revealed that the Indian heart-burning was not fortuitous.

The damage had already been done to India's big brotherly psyche. No sooner he arrived at the Tribhuvan International Airport, Dahal, as a step towards damage control, had announced before the press that looking at the special relationship we have with her the first destination for his political visit will be India. Is it a nose rubbing? If it is; such apologia, on purpose, denigrated nation's pride when the prime minister was needed to offer an explanation in the press not to read too much in his China visit and obliged to clarify where his first political visit would take place.

This indicates that the Maoist apparatchiks are novice in playing responsible politics and had failed to read the zeitgeist correctly. Dahal swallowed the Indian snub and had learnt his first lesson in the bilateral relation that it is indeed the dog wags the tail and not other way round, when India is the case.

The prime minister can run around the world on grand diplomatic tour when needed and it is his prerogative too. He can bask, while shaking hand with his counterparts, in the adulation of the country turning into republic. But he cannot hide from the fact that he has lost the turf in bilateral relation with India because of ultra-nationalist jingoism of the Maoists. It is a reminder to him that while dealing with issues of bilateral relation finesse is the order of the day and aggrandizement should be avoided if mutual trust is to be built.

No doubt the predicament is a serious setback to Nepal, yet I believe there is an alternative. Engagement and dialogue wherever possible always should have been our approach to achieving foreign affairs goal rather playing one card against other, a strategy of the hawkish elites of the monarchial period during the cold war era.

Renunciation, in Nepali politics particularly with communists, is a favored means to achieve one's desired end and the PM Dahal, true to its type, tried to play it out to perfection, but without result. When Foreign Minister Upendra Yadav was in Delhi for the BIMSTEC meeting, he met his Indian counterpart Pranab Mukherjee; while soothing the hurt Indian psyche he tried to convince his counterpart that Dahal's China visit was not at the cost of India's interest. While responding to Yadav on bilateral issues Mukherjee remained mute giving him short shrift in that topic. If this is any indication, it was a declaration of India's political line that China visit was a repudiation of the Indian benevolence.

While going to reinvent his ideological Guru, Mao-tse-Tung who has been exiled in souvenir shops, in Beijing the PM Dahal had hoped to reinvent himself. So, he changed the history route daring to chart an unconventional destination to redefine the historical legends. Unfortunately, his tradition-breaking journey turned into an internecine wrangle in the bilateral relation. His compulsion was understandable, but one does not need to travel all the way to China to renew one's nationalist perspective of sovereign country. Concatenation suggests that Maoist brinkmanship will cost Nepal one way or the other in future and to refrain from such burlesque to happen again let us avoid calling India's bluff.

When Dahal was rhapsodizing on the Mao's mausoleum and the Great Wall, the unprecedented Koshi flood was wreaking havoc on the eastern Terai leaving thousands of people in the lurch. The victims of flood were left without food and shelter and waiting for immediate salvage, while the Prime Minister Dahal was junketing in Beijing with his counterparts. Had he made a hasty retreat immediately after the closing ceremony of the Beijing Olympics, it would have assuaged the sufferings of flood victims, but he lost that chance in the afterglow of his political rise. Thus uncharitable portrait of Dahal as a ruthless commander of the PLA suddenly obtruded upon public psyche fearing what a new Nepal will look like in future, if the Maoists rule the roost.

Why did Dahal do it? And of the entire places in China? The most obvious explanation, of course, is he wanted to break the image trap that Nepal has – its politics is influenced by India and our leaders always toe the Indian line; that he is not a 'made in India' product and evinced to the domestic audiences that he is a tough guy and can take his decisions on his own. To disclose this emotion no other destination than China would be an alluring place for the political savvy demagogue. But he forgot that what might work at home does not necessarily play well across the boundary on the world stage. There is always a time and place to play brinkmanship.

Unfortunately, his tryst with Mao could not remain a smooth event as anticipated by the ultra radicals. What option has Dahal in his store to alter the strait-jacketed relationship with India? This is a challenge for him – to either submit to Indian hegemony by aligning with Indian expectations or to chart an independent course for New Nepal. His forthcoming visit to the land of Mahatma Gandhi will prove an indicator of Nepal government's mindset on the special relation that Dahal had talked about at the airport when he returned from China. It is, therefore, a much awaited visit for the political observers. This visit will unravel if Dahal, like his predecessors, will remain in rut or he can cudgel his brains.

The Kathmandu Post – September 3, 2008

44

Political Rumble-Tumble

Prudently Charting Out New Political Direction is Crucial

Finally, an oversized ego of the Maoists took its toll. The Maoist Prime Minister Pushpa Kamal Dahal, who went against the politics of consensus and unilaterally decided in the cabinet to retire the Chief of Army Staff (CoAS) Rookmangud Katawal from his position, had to pay by resigning from his post. Three coalition partners withdrew their support from the government and a lone ally also opposed the decision. Yet, the PM Dahal took the decision to remove the army chief. What an example of civilian supremacy!

If any further proof is needed about their intent to be a law onto oneself to effect their hidden agenda, the deliberate interference of the Maoists in bureaucracy, judiciary and the Nepal Army (NA) has provided it. Earlier, the PM Dahal's histrionics of seeking clarification from the army chief Katawal, in the make-believe reason of civilian supremacy, was nothing but an attempt to sack him before his term expires in September.

This, as is evident by now, brought a Tsunami in the mainstream politics. Seventeen political parties stood against the decision and charged the Maoist prime minister Dahal for his hunger for authoritarian dispensation and since then they have stalled the proceedings of the Constituent Assembly.

As the country watched the drama, there was tremendous pressure on the PM Dahal from inside and outside the country not to remove the CoAS. The Maoist hard-liners, however, remained adamant in their stand, so much so that the PM Dahal, unable to withstand the pressure, abstained from the May Day celebration in capital, a day which the brazen comrades normally celebrate with great pomp and splendor.

The Maoists leaders, ministers and the prime minister himself, ignoring the fact that they were leading a coalition government, went around the town claiming that the CoAS would be sacked no matter what. But, one of the major coalition partners, the CPN-UML, decided that the prime minister had right to seek clarification from the CoAS but removing him could only be done through consensus of all the political parties in the coalition.

This pushed the PM Dahal into a situation which was like riding a tiger ignorant of the knowledge on how to get off from it without being eaten.

When the President Ram Baran Yadav, the Supreme Commander of the Nepal Army, was forwarded the cabinet decision by the CoAS, he consulted with political parties and legal experts on this issue. Taking note of the unconstitutional decision of the cabinet, he wrote to the Council of Ministers to review its decision and later in the evening he instructed the CoAS Katawal to continue in his office as per the Interim Constitution, 2007 and the existing law. The president's action in the capacity of the guardian of the constitution stole all heat from the Maoist burlesque and rendered it a damp squib. Dahal's stint as prime minister for more than eight months was a sheer waste of time. The government formed with the single-point mandate of drafting the constitution, sadly, was not able to move an inch on that front.

The President Yadav's decision has put the Maoists in a quandary. The Maoist cadres were already chaffed at the failure of their leadership to deliver what he had promised. They still hark back to the days when their leaders had promised them wonderful dreams. Today that dream has been shattered and the leaders are simply looked upon as power wielders. Unless their leadership can integrate the Maoist combatants into the security forces, especially the NA, a large section of the party line is not going to believe the rhetoric of their leaders in the future while continuing to feel frustrated and cheated.

If the Maoist leadership can not contain the frustration insinuating into the psyche of their cadres, it will not be surprising if, in the coming days, more Rabindra Shresthas and Mani Thapas are born in the Maoist party. It seems that the going is getting tough everyday as the integration of the Maoist cadres is being delayed.

No doubt, the present standoff was unfortunate for everyone who believes in democracy. But, at the same time, our political parties must have learnt a lesson that only consensus is the way to move forward. Though the Prime Minister had time and again reiterated that this case too would be resolved through consensus but, much to the people's chagrin, he did not stand by his words and tried to take the people for a ride.

What new direction Nepali politics will take is of immense importance to everyone. If prudence prevails, we will see defense and strengthening of our multi-part democracy. If not, a drift into anarchy or a totalitarian system cannot be ruled out.

Repùblica – May 2009

45

Spot the Difference

As the general convention of the NC has kicked off and the election for its leadership is barely a day away as of this writing, there are no signs yet of who will emerge as its leader. The confused participants of the conclave are not yet clear about the would-be President because of factionalism in the party at every level. The stage is still wide open for deals, divorces and summer-saults. In the NC jamboree the three aspirants for the top job are trying to out-do each other. But observers find that none of the three has a serious agenda that could put him ahead of other two. Their harangues are all *cliché* ridden. Above all, none is inspirational or a role model who holds out hope for the future. The NC, which has always accepted the supremacy of genealogy above ideology, has run out of leaders with pan-Nepal appeal who could galvanize the nation and override ethnicity, religion and communal regionalism which has been the bane of our contemporary politics.

At a time when the NC is in desperate need of transformational leadership, all three candidates—the junior (Sushil) Koirala, Sher Bahadur Deuba and Bhim Bahadur

Tamang from the third front — are the extension of the legacy of the senior (Girija) Koirala and a manifestation of the NC leadership vacuum. The existence of none of the triumvirate could be imagined without the sheltering shadow of the Koirala dynasty. For junior Koirala his surname is his biggest ticket to power; for Deuba no price is too high when it comes to laying his claim to power. For Tamang conviction gives way to convenience when he reaches position of power. All the three enjoyed the dynastic privileges of Koirala but each has failed to get a foothold at the grassroots and been witnesses to the party's decline.

The third front, at the time of acute leadership crisis in the NC, is trying to find fresh and vibrant leaders with the capability to rope in members of all colours and hues. In this regard, observers had taken the third front as a logical evolution in the process of the NC's transformation. Even as it was looking for a maverick and dynamic personality, the proponents of the third front fielded Tamang as a stoic leader who lives Spartan life. No doubt, Tamang seemingly leads a simple life, yet there are many skeletons hidden in his closet. It remains a mystery why he and the candidates recommended by him failed in their electoral bids in 1990, at a time the Congress was at the top of Nepali politics. Why the front fell in with Tamang is a matter to delve into by the Congressites. But one thing is clear: the third front, in spite of its high-decibel ideological rhetoric, has to win the election and appease its cadres of different communities. It thus had to put up the face of *janajati* as a strategy.

The commitment paper (more like a manifesto) that Tamang and Narahari Acharya made public on August 26 is full of platitudes that every leader loves to reiterate but very few would like to dwell upon. When one looks at the worthies assembled under the banner of the third front, one is dismayed to find quite a number of infamous faces who have gained notoriety for manipulating the party and politics for their personal gains. For such leaders the utility of the third front is no more than a license for landing in the gallery of power. If this is the case, will the third front, however it fares in at the convention, be able to transform the NC to a party commensurate with the aspirations of the 21st century? If not, will it prove a prank on the part of its proponents?

During the NC's recent membership drive, an encouraging level of fresh blood has been infused in the party. This has given the NC well-wishers some hope that the party will finally be able to emerge from the rut. The new generation, thus, was optimistic about the third front: that it would prove a viable alternative to the geriatric leaders who are running the party at their whim. But when the third front announced Tamang's name for the president, it was a cold douche for these young Turks and grossly disappointed them not because they do not recognize Tamang's sacrifice – he was at concierge service of Koirala dynasty – yet he is not Koirala (senior) who had the persona to keep the party alive.

At a time when the NC is suffering from leadership vacuum, the third front should have had a much larger presence at the 12th general convention and given a distinctive impression that it has the capacity to reorient the party to face the challenges of domestic as well as international politics. For this to happen, its satraps need to develop a national appeal and shed their irrational arrogance of intellectual superiority so that the grassroots cadres could associate with them in a natural way.

Last but not the least, the one big idea that marks the change is missing in the third front. If it is the change that the Congress wants to be or the change that it wants to bring to the country, the third front has to reveal its mind with more clarity. The performance of its leaders is pretty dismal hitherto;

at no point could they convince the country that the third front is the change the NC has long been waiting for. If it indeed represents change, we are entitled to know in what ways it wants to bring it about.

The Kathmandu Post – September 21, 2010

46

Praxis of Evil

When Jhalnath Khanal was sworn in as the country's Prime Minister, I had heaved a sigh of relief, Thank God; at least camaraderie brought the two parties to their senses. My elation turned as a fleeting comfort when the events ensued thereafter. I felt ill at ease and sorry for the prime minister Khanal and the UCPN (M) chairperson Prachanda who had have been inexorably advocating the need of consensual politics for resolution of the existing political impasse. But their deeds fell far short their rhetoric when they signed a seven-point deal in *sub rosa* was unveiled. The deal was a peremptory declaration of the UCPN (M)'s *idée fixe* of the capturing of state power by any means possible.

Possibly, the country would not have witnessed bigger burlesques than this where both the comrades look like an old chestnut. Their repudiation on the CA's untimely demise seemed more like a consensual flirtation than it is a way towards consensus. The writer is reminded with the saying of Karl Marx, "History repeats itself, first as a tragedy and then as a farce." We saw the tragedy of Prachanda's term; and this time we are witnessing the farce of a dissembler prime minister. The seven-point deal they had signed resurrected the praxis of evil that was in vogue during the period of classical communism which is as authoritative and secretive as the Kremlin or the Forbidden City was in the heyday of Stalin or Mao.

When Khanal became the prime minister with the crutches of the UCPN (M), he told the press on the same day that he would give his cabinet a full shape in a week time. In spite of his whopping prank, he was pitting his wits against all odds to give his cabinet a full shape until a few days before he tendered his resignation to the president. His words proved a Dutch courage when he was unable to appoint a single minister even when seven days were past, let alone giving his cabinet a full shape. His party's central committee under his own chairmanship had decided not to give Home portfolio to the UCPN (M). He not only disregarded this decision rather went further and appointed ministers from his party without the party's approval. His presumptuous miffed the party's senior leaders like Nepal, Oli, and the general secretary Pokharel etc. and they took a pique against him. He was reprimanded in the party's meeting for his recalcitrance. His unilateral decisions were put before the disciplinary committee of the party for a probe. In order to cajole the UCPN (M) he even wielded his prime ministerial prerogative, but he failed to realize that his *Arjun Drishti* went totally out of sync when the peace process and statute drafting were left in cold. His move was more tactical than strategic as he was unable to look beyond the present.

Even his cabinet expansion for the third time did not bring stability to his government, yet it was his compulsion because he is aware of the fact that too long a wait can make him look stale. Across the nation, people kept asking – how long this government would remain floundering? While talking to the media Prime Minister Khanal looked hopeless as he was unable to bridge the chilling estrangement between the reality and the aspirations of his ally who is frozen in the language and style of the past.

In every coalition there involves a deal of give and take. Has the prime minister given more than he and his party received by signing the seven point agreement with Dahal? It is a topic for the UML to debate for the benefit of posterity. Both the UML and the UCPN (M) ignored the sentiment of people at large and therefore what was coming out was only their glib talks for public consumption.

Prachanda's withdrawal to support Khanal to be elected as the prime minister was the UCPN(M)'s strategy, but not its objective. It was apparently a message to India, whom he thinks a road-block to come to power, we can do what we like, come what may. In spite of his preening ego his wince was writ large when he was making his withdrawal address in the CA. He was visibly chafed by the candidature of Gacchadar and did not let loose the opportunity to stir up the communist Babel of foreign hand steeped in the pathology of anti-India psyche, a handy gizmo of radical communists in Nepal.

The leaders, although, they talk loud about consensus, they are not ready to lay off their claim for coveted ministries for deliberate reason. In the past, the Congress and the left parties had given leaders like B.P. Koirala, Pushpalal, Ganesh Man Singh, Madan Bhandari and others who could change the course of history with their slogan and transformational leadership. They were always driven by a sense of pride of nation. That was then. As our democracy grew older and is crossing its sixtieth year, such leaders are now an endangered species in our political landscape. Across the political parties of the nation, there is hardly a single leader with a visible national appeal, who could galvanize the nation, override ethnic, cast, and regional trivializations that have been a short-cut to the seat of power.

As the performance of the mainstream parties remained extremely opportunistic and lackluster, the verdict of the CA poll was coalition politics and consensus. This has boosted the ambitions of regional parties and their leaders to national prominence shrinking the influence of country's mainstream parties, the Congress, the CPN-UML, the UCPN-Maoist and others, in the country particularly in the Terai. At the moment nobody is sure how many such regional parties are in offing. Actually, the idea of regional parties is not bad in itself, giving voice to the genuine regional concerns at a time when nation is restructuring itself into a federal system. As we have seen here and elsewhere, such regional parties when steeped in ethnic, religious and communal hues, they become the breeding ground for Frankenstein monsters. The regional satraps should not be oblivious to this home truth.

When the UCPN-Maoist led government fell due to its preening egos, contradicting words and deeds, people looked to these regional parties for their decisive role. But these regional parties not only failed, proved unworthy of peoples' aspiration as well. While sustaining a coalition government the succour of such parties is essential, but their over-reach has earned indelible reputation of the necessary evils. This has developed a situation, where the government is not being run by mainstream parties; it is actually being dictated to by the fringes.

Because of the dramatic rise of regional parties in the national power equation, the regional players have developed super-sized egos which one notices unmistakably when these leaders meet with the media. After the resignation of the UCPN-Maoist led government, Upendra Yadav, the chairperson of the then undivided MJF which was in fourth position with fifty-three members in the CA, had laid his claim to form a government under the leadership of the Forum. This suggests that the regional leaders have grown disproportionately large in co-habitation politics aspiring to be kingmakers, if not kings.

Following the vertical split in the MJF, the Deputy Prime Minister Gachchadar had demanded his share of the spoils for his faction of the MJF in the form of key ministries. Until his demand is fulfilled he threatened not joining the government. But to keep themselves in the gallery of power they supported the coalition in the make-believe of lofty ideology. In reality, the ideology of these parties only a façade. If there is one, it plays second fiddle in the selfish pursuit of power.

To add insult to the injury, the Sadbhavana Party when they came to know that the Oil Corporation is detached from the ministry of Supply it annulled its previous decision only to join the cabinet later with a loss of face. TV channels had reported marathon meeting in Baluwatar and else where between these leaders to decide their share in the pie, but yet the Prime Minister Khanal's cabinet was not complete.

It is indeed an embarrassment to the Prime Minister for not being able to form his government even after passage of such a long period, because of the unrestrained demand of his alliance partners. This had pushed the Prime Minister into a situation where his cabinet grandees who were all dressed up but no office to go for some time. The selfish pursuit of power of the leaders have condescended Nepali politics to such a low that the meaning of conviction to them has lost for convenience. Not only have these leaders lost their face but miserably failed as well to convince common people that they care for us.

February 2011

47

Kitsch of Election

Preening Ego of the Prime Minister and his Allies Stymied the People's Right to Elect their Government

So it's all over again, and the sameness of the rigmarole is not only a repudiation of the failure of our political leaders unbound, it is also a display of their shameful lack of political will. The failure should be a cause for concern about their ability to deliver rising above the partisan interest at the time of crisis. Much to the chagrin of the highest office of the country, the President has been also dragged to watch the vaudeville helplessly. The disingenuous leaders every time made the President and the people believe that they are striving a consensual deal and would get one but every time it was the same old chestnut: groveling at the president for extension of the deadline.

The overwhelming banality of this open ended farce tells simple truth: either these leaders are inept in resolving the crisis manufactured by the Prime Minister Dr. Baburam Bhattarai's government or Nepalis are so complacent that we are not in hurry to get a constitution for our fledging republic and, so, we can wait till eternity.

Such unscrupulous action of our leaders has resulted in political slow bleed for the nation as the entire governance is running in an ad hoc basis. Positions in constitutional organs are falling vacant one after another. Political transition is irritatingly being overly stretched as the prime minister is not agreeing with his own party chairman's proposal setting his own riders. This has raised a serious question if the tail is wagging the dog or it is a prank for public consumption. The most charitable assessment of this rainbow coalition government of Dr. Babu Ram Bhattarai is that it has failed the people. Expectation has been steadily replaced by a blend of despair and cynicism. With their trendy talks and crafted looks, they are, as if, born for television and not for people's concern.

Political leaders who fail to address people's aspiration often store up problems for the future. Nepalis had voted in the CA election with an expectation to get a constitution of their aspiration that will unite the country, help in defining and elaborating a foresight of the future, transcend ethnic and religious divisions pursuing a strong national identity that will co-exist with regional affiliations.

But in the name of republic and the politics of identity, the UCPM and the Madhes-based parties tried to inculcating an ethnic and religious divide in Nepali psyche, thus propagating the Manichaeism of friends and enemies. The government of the UCPM and the UDMF headed by Dr. Baburam Bhattarai has instilled such lawlessness and culture of impunity in the society that every important institution that could have facilitated a consensual negotiation of the crisis thus stands destroyed. The government has taken political power not as a trust and responsibility bestowed upon them by the people but as a resource for personal ambitions and aggrandizement.

Ironically these leaders wasted the time of more than four years in political bickering and remained indulged in tongue lashing most of the time portraying one as holier than thou. While these leaders betrayed the nation and the people not delivering the constitution, the coalition government of Dr. Baburam Bhattarai, above all, cheated the people of their right to choose their government by not holding the election on November 22, 2012 as promised by him while he dissolved the CA without taking the opposition parties into confidence. Thus, it seems that dissolving the CA was the leitmotiv of Dr. Baburam Bhattarai's strategy to remain in power as a limpet. While Puspa Kamal Dahal alias Prachanda, the Chairman of his party, is slogging at the formation of a consensual government to shorten the transitional situation, Prime Minister Bhattarai and his coalition partners are throwing spanner into Dahal's effort. Because of such ambivalence proviso of Dr. Bhattarai, the going has got tough not only to the opposition parties but for his chairman Prachanda as well. This has excoriated an intractable power struggle between them in the UCPM, an inevitable destiny of communist party.

After a long wait Nepalis were given a hope that a consensual deal is at the doorstep. But the latest rider of the Prime minister and the UDMF proved a cold douche on the efforts of the political parties trying for a consensual deal and raised a question mark: do the government of the UCPM and the UDMF sincerely want the election in April-May? The Prime minister is well-aware of the fact that if the government of national consensus does not come into existence, neither the constitution making process will advance further nor the election that is being much touted by the Prime Minister could be held. Except the leap service the government is not doing any serious effort, which is visible on board, to hold the election rather playing a blame game, a favorite pastime of comrades.

Tough messages are easier to send and the Prime Minister Dr. Bhattarai's one such *cliché* ridden rant, he would not succumb to opposition's demand unless a package deal is accepted, is unlikely to be heeded under the situation of distrust and act of filibuster. He can bask, while going remains favorable, in the glow of his tough message, but he cannot hide from the fact that he has lost the plot at home when he revealed that the key of Nepali politics is not with him rather lies somewhere else. After the exposé of this bitter truth, people firmly believed that the Prime Minister Bhattarai is using the kitsch of holding the election by the elected government is like a drunken man uses a lamp post for support rather than illumination.

Now the UCPM and the parties of the UDMF no longer inspire people at large, when they see the ideology of the parties is no longer for commitment but for convenience. Not only their popularity is sliding but opinion on their leadership is also divided. From the Prime minister to the ministers, all have invariably failed in endurance test of their integrity. How could such a bunch of flunkies hold the much touted election fair and free from fear and intimidation? The cruelest irony of today's Nepali politics is: the government of Dr. Baburam Bhattarai is not part of the consuming crisis but it has been conducting itself as part of the solution, which is not true.

In order to guarantee the right of the people to choose their government, the President, as the guardian of the interim constitution, needs to come forward and explore a government of non-political citizens to conduct the election free and fairly. Of course, such move is not possible unless the political parties are taken into confidence. Such action will not only exonerate the stigma of foreign intervention in Nepali politics but also from the scathing blame – government formation of any party here is not possible unless foreign power signals green light.

Telegraphnepal.com – December 30, 2012

48

Madhes is Not Just A Geography, It is A Microcosm of Ethnic Harmony

The Hill and Terai divide, a geographical disparate perverted to ethnic division, has turned as a totemic pole of the Madhesi political parties. It is the result of angry faith of hate against the hegemony of the Pahade, a synonym of ruling elites, than the Madhes redemption. This Madhesi anxiety exaggerated by demographic arrogance that has set off the Madhes agitation of 2006 was, as the Madhesi leaders assert, for establishing the Madhesi identity in the national mainstream. But the paradox was they turned the 'divide' into Manichean division of friends and enemies with predilection to ethnic hatred for gaining the political mileage. The Madhesi emotion retrieved from the movement later swerved by its leaders to the Pahade bashing, much to the delight of the regressive communal forces. With such perforated delight the Madhes is still in struggle to redeem from politics of paranoia.

But person like me who was born and brought up there more than sixty years ago, it was a painful example of racial politics at its atavistic worst. The Madhesi leaders had flaunted it as a triumphant moment of the Madhesi militancy oblivious of unleashing the pathology of distrust in our multi-ethno society that has visibly smashed the very fabric of communal harmony into smithereens in the Terai. For the community that is under siege, it was the vindication of the Madhesi hate against the Pahade stage-managed by the tyranny of demographic arrogance that forced them to migrate to the safer places abandoning their birth place in a great pain.

There is another burlesque the Madhes has been witnessing: for its leaders, those seasoned ventriloquists who came from across the border at different intervals of time are the sons of the soil but those who are born and lived there along with them from generations wax unbecoming residents. These parachuted-faceless sons of the soil-turned voters, they excel in absurdities only, they have nothing at stake, except, a few borrowed slogans to keep the communal pot boiling.

Despite high decibel rhetoric during the agitation, no Madhesi leaders ever showed gumption to their Pahade counterparts to stop them to migrate from their birth places, the Madhes, in the sheer blatancy of vote-bank politics. When one reads the statements of these leaders at that time who were competing each other in spewing out hate against the Pahade, the message was loud and clear. This suggests that Nepal has always remained the biggest incomprehension of the Madhesi leaders and they are woolly-headed to vouch if their umbilical cord is attached here or anywhere else. Their denial to cooperate to update the voter-list is the same old chestnut: though, they do not say so, one still gets the feeling that everyone coming from other side of the border should be accepted as Nepali citizen. The logical extension of such polemic is: the Madhesis are willing to live with illegal migrants from across the border but not ready to accept the Pahade denizens in the Terai.

The new lexis of the Madhesi liberation has made the jock further conceited – there are several well educated Madhesis who have had been enjoying all the perks and privileges that the State provides to its nationals, but yet flippantly remark in public platform that they are here as a second class citizen living in internal colonial rule. If it is true, Nepal then is hell for them and the Pahade have made them Nepalis redundant. In all fairness one must accept that this is a warped view of the Madhesi psyche not to believe in meritocracy. If they believe in open, competitive and pluralistic society, they must accept the fact that the country will be better off when the best beats the rest.

They are in the gallery of power all the time; yes, not in the centre of power. And, this is not because they are the Madhesi, rather the home truth is, a modicum of education, societal awareness and development level of the Madhesi society is the *raison d´être* for their predicament. They need to be bold enough and sincere to accept the truth. As their society opened up and awareness level enhanced, the power of clerisy has increased bringing them more opportunities to play vital roles not only in the state's affairs but in the Nepali society as a whole. Therefore, sooner they recognize the incontrovertible fact 'the best must succeed' and stop grappling with reservation, inclusion, priority right, etc. as backdoor entry, earlier the Madhesi society and the nation, in general, will prosper.

Although, the Madhes agitation, has semaphored the Madhesi political parties to power, there is no denying the fact that the empowered leaders failed to turn the Madhes a peaceful place to live in for their own community. In recent years, I was surprised to see several of my Madhesi friends hanging around in the capital during the Dashain, Diwali and Chhat festival due to fear of intimidation and extortion in the Terai. What does it signify? When your means are foul and disingenuous, definitely the end you meet will be delirious. The deceitful slogan of these shenanigans, *one Madhes one Pradesh* appeared emotional *albeit*, it was not the Madhes redemption; it is more ethnic than pan Terai sentiment and does not include the communities that live there from generations. Such ethnic divide has transformed the Terai in a playing field for illegal armed groups and extortionists. Today's Madhes is riddled with such Frankenstein.

As things are precipitating in the Terai, keeping politics aside, its denizens are coming out of reverie and sincerely acknowledging the contribution made by their Pahade counterparts, who are born and lived there from generations, in bringing the Terai's development to today's state. Such redressal will help to build confidence between the two communities and pump fresh dynamism to the jaded mindset. They also opine that the mushrooming Madhesi parties failed to bring the massive reform that are needed to transform their medieval society. It is, therefore, high time that these leaders should show courage to stand up and tell our community why they have performed so poorly even when the political landscape was conducive for such initiatives. Further, they should show their sagacity to bring their Pahade counterparts into confidence. Such a move might bring a new era of accountability and act as a succor in healing the purported humiliation of ethnic divide. Let us hope that the revulsion spawning in the Madhes among general Madhesis should act as devil's advocate to the leaders to revisit their agenda of their respective parties.

Most Madhesi liberals observe that the swirl storm of 2006 has lost its emotive force due to internal wrangling among the Madhesi parties. The number of the Madhesi parties suggests that the Madhesi leaders will not remain behind their communist counterparts in splitting it. The latest split in the sequel is the Sadbhavana Party (Rajendra Mahto) again. As a political issue it has yielded diminishing returns for them but yet they will not refrain from further division.

In the Terai people in general are in doubt that these leaders can uphold the Madhes agenda, because of their clannish feud and I-me-myself culture inculcated in their psyche. These liberals think, "Our leaders should stop making fuss of voter-list updating procedure, as there are several other issues that need attention for development of the Madhes and its society. Instead, our leaders are as limpets looking for power only. Life in the Madhes, though, looks as usual it is far from normal. In recent times more and more Madhesis are becoming the victims of manufactured violence perpetrated by our own community." While listening to them one can not miss a sense of angst in their voices of concern.

Nobody is judging these leaders' credentials in this respect. Perhaps, their unwieldy declarations as one Madhes one Pradesh, bulk entry of ten-thousand Madhesi youth in the Nepal army, etc. have become the mantras of apologias. One cannot deny the discrimination meted out to the communities of the Madhes, but it is also true that such parochial outlook is not reparation either. As if being a concerned Madhesi is nothing but being loud, exhibitionistic, self-righteous and anti-Pahade. This psyche has not only hindered the development of culture of holding informed discourses, it has also given birth to a mindset that explains if you criticize a Madhesi leader (even based on facts) it is a mud-slinging and a part of conspiracy theories, a way to prove one's credential as a Madhesi *Messiah*.

The axe fallen on the Pahade community that dispelled them from the Terai has been used on the Madhesi themselves by the flunkeys who flaunt themselves as members of one or another political parties or armed groups of the Madhes. *Tu quoque*! Not only it has put the political parties of the Madhes in a spot, the scathing situation developed in the Terai is pressurizing them for introspection of their Madhes policy in the national context of totality. Thus, these parties are caught in a catch 22 situation where they cannot abandon their core political rhetoric that is associated with their identity issue as the Madhes-based parties. If ever these parties contemplate a makeover commensurate with the zeitgeist of 21st century, the issue of *one Madhes one Pradesh* will keep hovering in the minds of the Madhesi leaders like a spectre that has not been exorcized.

Telegraphnepal.com – June 7, 2013

49

Faint Hope

"Not taking a decision is also a decision," said the late PV Narshimha Rao, former Prime Minister of India. One wonders if the same has been a guiding principle for our leaders currently engaged in constitution making.

Constituent Assembly is in a pause now. The blasé attitude of our political leaders has let people down since the CA was first formed in 2008. They have been repeating platitudes on timely statute but when the deadline nears they harp on why, failing consensus, there could be no agreement. For these leaders consensus has become an excuse to prolong transition.

Constitution drafting has been sluggish due to lack of trust and Machiavellian politics our leaders have championed. They have used 'consensus' as a bargaining chip to fulfill their vested interests and push for ethnic states, right to self-determination and 'One Madesh One Province' demand, among others. The recent protest rally by the Federal Republic Front (FRF) in the capital shows the self-serving leaders of the alliance still have a potential to hurt and further destabilize the transitional politics.

When the UCPN (Maoist) chairman Pushpa Kamal Dahal was made coordinator of the High Level Political Committee, it had inspired some hope. The HLPC was meant to facilitate consensus and create an atmosphere of trust among parties. But Dahal has proved that the whole drama of obstructing the House was nothing but a step to elevate him to the HLPC chair. His address to the FRF rally in the capital on October 17 indicates the same.

The FRF comprises of 22 parties, and most from them were rejected by voters in the CA II polls. They have threatened to launch a fresh revolt if constitution is drafted without taking them into confidence. The same Dahal who demanded the HLPC for the constitution seems bent on derailing the process. Delivering such whopper is nothing new for Dahal, whose track record of deceitfulness has been proved by the Shaktikhor videotape and Katuwal episode. But he has no right to put the statute process in limbo.

When you don't want to arrive at solutions, problems cannot be solved. If you are not ready for compromise, consensus becomes far cry. The FRF leaders are trying to defy solution by opposing voting process. Their cliché-ridden war-cry is not only against the spirit of consensus but also undermines the mandate of the CA II polls.

If memory serves us right, all these leaders during the CA II election had committed that the constitution would be drafted by consensus and if there cannot be consensus, the constitution will be decided by voting. Dahal, while campaigning during the CA II election, had committed to the same. It is unfortunate that he is backtracking from this commitment. It is a great betrayal to Nepalis who voted in the CA II polls believing that the leaders would deliver the constitution this time, through consensus or voting. It is an insult to people not to allow the majority of their representatives to decide the constitution. Dahal's ferocious speech at the FRF rally also shows that he still believes offence is the best defense.

Leaders behave irrationally often when they exhaust all options, just like Dahal and the FRF leaders. They have resorted to jingoism and vigilantism to justify their arguments. Nepalis love their country but that does not give anyone the right to ignore the verdict of more than tow-third of voters. Notwithstanding shifting priorities of our selfish leaders, I still hope, they will surprise us and the world in the end.

Repùblica – October 29, 2014

50

The Kitsch of Civilian Supremacy

The telecast of the video footage by several TV channels, showing the PM Pushpa Kamal Dahal Prachanda's more than an hour long harangue to his PLA combatants at the Shaktikhore Camp on January 2, 2008, not only put the Maoist rank and file out of humour, it has queered the Maoist pitch to rule the roost also. While beholding the video tape one is inclined to conjecture the cold fact that it is only a tip of iceberg and there could be many more skeletons hidden in his closet. Because of such ruse on the part of the Maoists, the PM Dahal being at his apogee has to step down from the position of premiership. The general public retort is *tu quoque*.

We had, in general, an impression that Nepalis are quite a good judge of people. This belief was further justified when we saw the result of the constitution assembly (CA) election, particularly at the time when general public is disenchanted with leaders of political parties because of their ineptitude and me-my family-I attitude. Everybody had expected that the Maoists will prove itself of a different metal. But with the telecast of the appalling video footage where Prachanda was talking bestially about his party's apple-cart to capture the state power by politicizing the Army through the PLA integration and channeling huge sum of public money under various pretext from the state resources for making their battle plan. I then realized how wrong Nepalis were while judging the Maoists during the CA poll when voted them as a single largest party to draft the new constitution of the fledgling republic.

Political parties, international community and everyone who had given them a benefit of doubt looked askance at the Maoist's sincerity to the peace process after watching this video. The World Bank has raised a serious concern about the reality of the inflated number of the PLA combatants before reimbursing the government its committed grant assistance under the emergency peace support programme (ESPS). Prachanda has betrayed the people's trust by his bland persona. The only cold comfort is they have fooled many people including international community and the UN who should have known them better. What bigger parody can there be when the Prime Minister Prachanda, addressing the UN general assembly, was ostentatiously talking about bringing the on going peace process in the country to its logical conclusion while at the same time he and his party had a hidden agenda of capturing the state power up their sleeves.

The brunt of the videogate scam falls on the UNMIN also along with others who are involved in the verification process. Ian Martin, the then chief of the UNMIN, needs to clarify if it had missed the truth because he has soft corner for them or has been dodged by the Maoists. Under both the situations it is the dereliction of the chief and his entire crack team and the rest of the members. How the UNMIN corrects this slip-up will, without doubt, bear upon the strength and the integrity of the Maoists. It is too early to guess how the Maoists will respond to the UNMIN's correction, if it does one, although they are with the stuffing knocked out of them at present.

The present political crisis is the result of ambivalent perception of the Maoists with an oversized ego. The resignation of the PM Dahal from his position is due to the crisis of his own making when he failed to take his coalition partners along. With the post-crisis political situation, release of the videotape has taken sheen out of the Maoists and turned him from *avant garde* to a desperado. Above all, while he was still a caretaker Prime Minister, pushing all diplomatic norms and political ethics at bay, he contemptibly blamed the president's salvation move as a *coup d'état*. Utterly disregarding the aspirations of the interim constitution, the political consensus, he indulged in scathing of the President to justify his veiled intention of installing a totalitarianism capturing the state power. Thus, his fall from grace, although, was as surreal for him but it was inevitable in terms of public image.

When the President Ram Baran Yadav stymied his move to divide and politicize the Army, Prachanda's wince was writ large during the hurriedly called press conference and also while addressing the meeting of the Society of families disappeared by the State in the capital. His paroxysm during his address was Prachanda unbound and it was a repudiation of the prime ministerial dignity and its onus. He was visibly chafed and did not let loose the opportunity to stir up the communist Babel of anti-Indian psyche, a handy gizmo of Nepali communists to reach the helm of power.

Maoists, for this matter all communists, in Nepal have a tendency to define an Indian help/advice according to their convenience – cooperation or an intervention. They would not hesitate even to look a gift-horse in the mouth. Such was the scene in the Maoists' protest meeting at the *Khula Manch* on Sunday when the PM Dahal without naming any one spewed diatribes against India. But he was oblivious to the fact that when he and his comrades were running for their lives, it was India's succour that provided them a safe heaven in Noida (Delhi) during the so-called Peoples' War.

Nepalis are aware of the fact that some of the European countries are supporting the Maoists to the hilt morally and financially. This has been vindicated by the visit of the Prime Minister, Prachanda to those countries without serious business agenda. After the disclosure of the Maoists' intention through the video footage what these countries, who advocate democracy and human rights in international arena, have to say. Nepalis are waiting to hear them, as the general feeling of the people here is that these countries are accomplices in the Maoist apple-cart in one way or other. If this is not true, they should dare to renounce the Maoists' anti-people stratagem as exposed by the videotape display and stop their largesse incognito.

Since the reality has come to the fore now, it is interesting to watch how these countries and the donor organizations respond to the siphoning of huge sum of money by the Maoist party from donors' committed assistance to buy arms with an intention to capture the state.

The pretext of civilian supremacy, the PM Dahal invented for his resignation, has been torpedoed by the vedeogate scam. He has not only fooled the citizens of the country, but also robbed them of their hard-earned tax money to buy arms for his PLA fighters. Taking people for a ride is the same old chestnut of the Maoist party, which they do not intend to remorse. It seems that Prachanda has obviously paid heed to Nazi propaganda of Joseph Goebbles who said, "If you tell a lie big enough and keep repeating, people eventually come to believe it." But Nepalis believe that truth ultimately prevails. Therefore, after the exposé of the videotape Nepalis from different walks of life are of the opinion that the PM Prachanda used the pretext of civilian supremacy like a drunken man uses a lamp-post for support rather than illumination.

May 2009

51

Repatriation or Expatriation?

Refugee Rigmarole on the Last Shangri-La

Introduced as often the Last Shangri-la, Bhutan is familiar abroad through two sources. One is Kuensel, a newspaper and online, the official mouthpiece of the Royal government of Bhutan (RGB), which does not tire of harping on the Gross National Happiness (GNH) while a large part of its population subsists below the poverty line. It is silent on how the population figure registered as 1.3 million, including the Lhotshampas, in the United Nations during its admission in 1971 declined to a little over 0.6 million. If the RGB can not explain this reduction, how could people believe in its claim to be a Shangri-la?

The other source through which we come to know about Bhutan is people like Tek Nath Rijal and Thinley Penjore struggling hard for the repatriation of their fellow refugees. These men of conviction have lived in Bhutan, dreamt of Bhutan and endured Bhutan, amidst the hopelessness of an endless journey of refugee life and now stuck between the two horns of a dilemma: should they still stand for repatriation, or should they abandon the whole mission in favour of expatriation?

1. Rediscovering the Roots of the Crisis

This rigmarole makes the refugee issue not only one of the most protracted issues of the region, but it is also probably the most neglected in the world at large. Living in the camps of south-eastern Nepal, they do not see an immediate end to their ordeal. Exceeding one hundred thousand in number, they are mostly Nepali speaking Lhotshampas. Although, in small numbers, other ethnic groups like Ngalongs, Sarchops, Khengs also constitute the pool of the refugee community. These refugees have lived all or most of their lives in Bhutan, but they fled or were forcibly evicted from their homes in Bhutan in 1990 when the RGB introduced a highly discriminatory citizenship policy targeting the ethnic Nepalis, particularly those critical of the government policy.

Ruled by a hereditary autocratic King, Bhutan has continuously denied recognition to the refugees as Bhutanese nationals. The RGB claims that the refugees are non-Bhutanese people or are voluntary migrants who gave up their citizenship rights voluntarily while departing. Taking world community for a ride, the RGB wants them to believe that its own citizens, who number in thousands, voluntarily abdicated their citizenship rights. But it remains silent on why such a large number of its population would ever agree to relinquish the natural right of their citizenship. The tragic stories of these refugees, narrated and published several times, eloquently testify to the sinister design of the RGB to coerce and torture the people at gun point to leave their homes by signing the Voluntary Migration Form.

Yielding to the international pressure, Bhutan reluctantly agreed to sit with Nepal on bilateral talks and after several rounds of joint ministerial level (JML) talks, the two governments agreed to a joint status verification and categorization process as a precursor to repatriation. But Bhutan skillfully played with Nepal making inconsistent statements every time the talks were scheduled. In the course of verification and categorization of the refugees, the key victims of the crisis, were never consulted. As a host country, Nepal should have facilitated the verification process and allowed the refugees to face the Bhutan team directly. Since it could not, the RGB has been able to gain an upper hand.

The procrastinatory stance adopted by the RGB shows that Nepal made a mistake in agreeing to Bhutan's proposal.

The Indian apathy towards the refugee problem is another piece in the puzzle. It has encouraged the RGB to intensify ethnic cleansing. India has always maintained that it is a bilateral concern of Nepal and Bhutan, whereas, the whole world knows that India cannot brush its hands off the issue, as the refugees could not have been transported to Nepal without the involvement of the government of India. It is thus obvious that without the participation of India the refugee crisis can not be resolved. It is high time now for India to play a pro-active role in solving this crisis.

Under the changed political circumstances, Nepal must revisit its approach and adopt a policy of 'Advocacy, Diplomacy and Lobbying' (ADL) rather than acquiescence.

2. Unwanted, Unwelcome

The RGB's decision to exile its citizens may look at first fortuitous. A closer look, however, will show it is a well thought design to marginalize the Lhotshampas, which were exerting a profound influence on the Bhutanese life and the body politique there. Ethnic cleansing was started to counter that influence.

When Sikkim was annexed to India in 1975 by the support of Nepali population, and later when the Gorkha National Liberation Front (GNLF) raised its voice for a separate Nepali state in the Indian Union, the Druk government feared a repeat of such events. But Indira Gandhi, who was then the Prime Minister of India, assuaged Bhutan's anxieties telling it had nothing to fear.

However, the royal government remained askance at the Nepali-speaking community. Because of their growing population and level of awareness, they formed political parties and called for democratic rights which were perceived as a threat by the rulers.

The events of Sikkim and the GNLF movement, moreover, offered the excuse to the RGB for its ethnic cleansing, eliminating threat from Nepali-speaking population in the future.

The premiership of Rajiv Gandhi, when the relation between Nepal and India was at its lowest ebb and the Gorkhaland movement in West Bengal was at its zenith; brought the opportunity to the king he had been probably looking for long. Consulting with India on the fate of the Lhotshampas, the king annulled the 1958 Citizenship Act and promulgated another one in 1985 with stringent requirements for obtaining and retaining citizenship. The new act also included the provision for revocation of citizenship in case of "disloyalty" to the king and the country, an excuse the RGB used arbitrarily to denationalize large number of the Lhotshampas when it carried out the census in southern Bhutan in 1988. Reports were rife that under the direction of Thimpu the local government officials had made arbitrary census classifications to dislodge the Nepali-speaking community from Bhutan.

The RGB further introduced the Bhutanization measures such as "One Nation, One People" in 1989 which forced people to adopt the dress code and the termination of Nepali language in schools. In early 1990, ethnic Nepalis and others had protested by organizing large public demonstrations and forming political parties calling for multi-party democracy.

The bell had begun tolling for the Thimpu's regime and the RGB came heavily upon the demonstrators as the Bhutanese police and army imprisoned, raped, and tortured to death many who were associated with the demonstration.

Thousands of people fled or were forced to leave by 1992. But before they crossed the border, the RGB forced many also to sign the "Voluntary Migration Form" to surrendering their rights to Bhutanese citizenship.

3. Negotiations Fail

After the arrival of Bhutan's refugees, the Nepal government settled them in the camps with the assistance of the UN and donor agencies wanted to open a dialogue with the Bhutanese government. However, from the very beginning, the RGB avoided talking about the refugees contending they were not Bhutanese nationals. It was only later that it finally agreed to do it after tremendous international pressure was mounted.

Since, the first bilateral talk between Nepal and Bhutan in 1993, nearly sixteen rounds of meetings have been held only to get nowhere. To eschew censure from the international community Bhutan does skillfully engage itself in the bilateral talks, but it never loses a single opportunity to delay or cancel the meeting whenever possible.

The first "verification process" of 12,500 refugees in the Khudunabari camp by the joint team on 14 December 2001 revealed the presence of 75% Bhutanese there. The shocked RGB remained silent for a year or so. Pressure was mounting and the Bhutanese team took two years to announce their decision on the verification results, but with a preemptive strategy to derail the process. The team, moreover, used abusive language provoking the so-called scuffle. Unable to face the refugees, and abandoning all diplomatic norms, the Bhutanese team left in a huff without even informing the host country.

All efforts made by the RGB to manipulate the incidence to garner international support and sympathy had thus come to naught. Clumsy diplomacy brought it a certain loss of face; as a result Bhutan since 2003 has turned its back to the whole verification process and has been resisting every effort by Nepal to bring it to the negotiation table.

4. Road to No-Where

That Nepali diplomacy has failed and failed miserably on the Bhutan front is there for everyone to see. No less evident is the fact those sixteen years of ordeal, over a dozen rounds of talks and twelve months of verification process turned out to be an empty rigmarole for unfortunate refugees down a road to nowhere. The failure was writ large in Nepal's offer to provide citizenship to the refugees. The decision was not just unfortunate it signaled the collapse of Nepal's diplomacy itself.

The failure lay not only in the inability of the government in Kathmandu tc consult with the refugee leaders, but also in its inability to educate the international community on the issue. Why did not Nepal even once ask India to intervene? Obviously, could the refugees have crossed the border sans Indian "assistance"? And, why did not Kathmandu protest when its Border Security Forces dumped them on this side of the border in collaboration with the Bhutan's security forces? Clearly tripartite issue was paraded as a bilateral one, and the diplomacy of Kathmandu had failed by conceding at this point to.

All these failings fetched gains for Thimpu which could not but capitalize on the opportunities Nepal offered. Internal unrest in Nepal had spread nationwide and Thimpu used the predicament to outwit the ruling regime every time it could – by protracting the talks or otherwise. By the time Kathmandu realized Thimpu's conspiracy, it was too late: conceded to all the proposals scripted by Bhutan.

There is neither a cell to monitor the refugee situation in the Foreign Ministry or in the Home Ministry, nor a mechanism yet to review the state's policy on the issue. As a consequence, the government is unable to get any expert inputs into the refugee strategy in its home work.

In Nepal, the government's policy changes like weather, as ministers are changed, spawning discontinuity and inconsistency and dithering claims. Adhocism in handling the refugee issue is the natural consequence evident in the erratic statements, of the prime minister, foreign minister and other leaders on the issue of third-country resettlement.

5. The Shadow that Hovers

The refugee crisis is not merely a humanitarian issue but also a much broader problem related to the democratization of a whole nation and its people. For, unless the refugee problem is politically addressed, people there can not live a dignified life. Repatriation alone, minus political changes may bring more harm than benefit, evicting thousands of Bhutanese in the name of illegal migrants, non-nationals, anti-nationals, and criminals. This is not a mere figment of some one's mind. For, aware of Achilles hill in Nepal's diplomacy and its proven inability to influence India so far, Bhutan is said to be preparing itself to evict another 60-70 thousand Bhutanese people, pro-democracy supporters or those involved in political activities directly or indirectly.

Thus raises the question, what should Nepal do for the safety of the Nepali-speaking people there? Should it remain silent or should it take up the matter with India to preempt the Bhutanese move?

Role of India is becoming crucial in more than one way. Its silence so far has, certainly, not helped. In fact, had it not been India, the refugees would not have landed in Nepal and contiguity to Bhutan would have kept them inside India itself.

Bilateralising a trilateral crisis hardly will make a dent and will only protract the issue, but protracting a crisis is hardly the rational strategy, as Palestinian crisis shows. Allowing the conflict to fester further will invite more problems in the future not only for India, Bhutan and Nepal, for the whole region as such.

In the context, the proposal to resettle the refugees in a third-country could well look like timely relief for many at first, but is it really one? The proposal pushes the political dimension of the issue – democracy and human rights – into oblivion. The governments offering settlement have failed to take account of the impending backlash to another 60-70 thousands of Bhutanese declared as non-nationals by the RGB, mostly the kith and kin of the refugees and political dissidents living abroad. If not carefully examined, the offer may start another wave of exodus from Bhutan. Is that what the International community wants?

Under the pretext of democratization, a new constitution has just been drafted by a committee of 39 members. It is not difficult to anticipate what will follow when at least one-fifth of its population is in exile and the drafting committee represents none except a few hand picked apparatchiks. The democratic constitution is a clear eye-wash, an effort to hoodwink the world at large, to sustain the desperate regime. The mock election, just held as a familiarization exercise, is only a prelude to disfranchise the refugees in the elections slated for 2008.

6. Reigniting the Spirit of the Movement

Had it been a humanitarian issue alone, the refugee crisis would not have lingered for so long. When several rounds of bilateral talks did not yield any result, the refugee leaders organized a long Dharna in front of the UN and the SAARC office in Kathmandu. The Dharna, drew the world's attention to the issue stirring public conscience both inside and outside the country. As a result, the international community began to visit refugee leaders and camps, which was clearly an embarrassment for the UN, involved in coordinating the donors' help, and for the SAARC as well, whose Director General happens to be from Bhutan, but who had declined even to receive the memorandum from the refugees.

7. What Needs to be Done

In order to resolve the issue, Nepal needs to reconsider its approach and change its track. A robust strategy of ADL on the theme is what needed one that must be pursued actively and consistently. The agenda must now assume the priority it has failed to get so far, and the solution sought must be a permanent one. Tackling the problem will demand quite a few measures some of which are:

1. In order to deal with all aspects of the refugee issue in its entirety, a High Level Task Force needs to be formed on a permanent basis until an amicable solution is reached. The body can provide inputs to the government in a continued manner, so that the government can formulate strategies and policies for short, mid and long in course of negotiation.

2. Nepal must immediately nullify the bilateral talks.

3. Kathmandu must try to convince India to enter the negotiation process, so that tangible decisions can be made to resolve the issue.

4. Nepal should press for the representation of the refugee leaders and the UN in the negotiation. Since the representative nature of the Bhutanese Movement Steering Committee (BMSC) allows it to function as the mouthpiece of the Bhutanese refugees, the government of Nepal should recognize the BMSC as a nodal body to represent the refugees' interest.

5. Refugees should be divided only into two categories – Bhutanese and non-Bhutanese, in place of the existing

four-fold categorization, that is nothing but to render thousands of refugees stateless.

6. In case trilateralization does not help, Nepal should take the matter to the international community.
7. The policy of Advocacy, Diplomacy and Lobbying (ADL) in international platform needs to be intensified.

The political history of Bhutan hides a certain cruel irony in it: marginalization of a whole mass that has contributed in many ways to the development of Bhutan. There came a moment in its history – in the early part of the last century – when someone of Nepali origin played a crucial role in its existential stake, apart from the role of thousands of Nepalis in the opening and development of the Duars. What could be, therefore. more agonizing to them than their present predicament: exile from the rulers, neglect from the region, connivance from the world body and isolation from the world at large?

Dictionary defines expatriation as withdrawal from residence in or allegiance to own's native country. The dilemma the Lhotshampas face today is no less agonizing. If they agree for expatriation en masse, they will become a party to the ugly specimen of aid to prostitute a noble mission. Abandoning that mission will not only bring to naught the suffering and martyrdom of many who have fought for a certain cause, to pursue an easy life abroad, but also to betray the process of democratization of that nation. It is, of course, for the refugees and their leaders to decide what is to be done. But in any decision that they now take, they must think through long enough and well enough on the two options that stare at them today: Repatriation or Expatriation?

The paper was presented in the round table meeting organized by the Institute of Foreign Affairs (IFA) in May 21, 2007 (Kathmandu, Nepal).

Development Issues

52

Plight of Agricultural Research System

In its revised agricultural statistics, the National Planning Commission (NPC) reported an agricultural growth rate of 2.30 percent a year for food-grains and 2.20 percent for cash-crops over the period 1980/81 to 1990/91. By comparison, the population growth rate for the same period was 2.5 percent a year. The sluggish growth rate of the agricultural sector has taken its toll, pushing the country from a regular net exporter of food-grains to a modest importer in recent years. The "below the mark" performance of this sector is a matter of concern to policymakers, planners and agricultural scientists alike. A dispassionate analysis of the functioning of the institutions related to agricultural development activities is needed. These include agricultural research, extension, education, support services (irrigation, inputs, credit-market, etc.) and above all, government policies and actions that shape these institutions and gear them towards their present state of affairs.

Agricultural research is the engine that drives the economic process by increasing production many-folds through the application of improved technologies generated by research. Without effective client oriented agricultural research suited to the needs of the country, an increase in the agricultural growth rate is simply not possible.

An effective output oriented National Agricultural Research System (NARS) is a precondition to sustain increased productivity in the long run. With this view, the NARC was established in the county after the restoration of democracy. Efforts to create an autonomous NARS continued for almost a decade. Finally, the government took appropriate action by approving the National Agriculture Research Council (NARC) Act 1991 to streamline the apex institution that can positively influence agricultural scientists. But it only half-heartedly supported the new institution.

There were instances when the Ministry of Agriculture stepped beyond its authority to order the NARC to change its rules and regulations in the name of a minister's wish. Ever since its birth, the NARC has persistently been pushed into controversies to show that such autonomous institution simply cannot function in Nepal. If the institution is necessary at all, these critics argue, the chief of the institution should be nominated from outside the system, preferably from the government bureaucracy. Frequent changes in appointees to the NARC governing board and to the varied leadership positions in the NARC at the will of the minister have aggravated the situation immensely. This was, after all, a grand design of the anti NARC lobby, which does not want the NARC to function independently.

Through the years, the NARC has been seriously plagued and paralyzed by this political maneuvering and over-ridden with the inherent problems of a partisan game of musical chairs with little time to carry out its mandated work. In fact, internally, the NARC is in nothing short of total disarray – close to being in a complete mess. Partisan politics is rampant and research managers and scientists have become easy pawns of political interest. Enough is enough – the game must stop.

All along, every NARC leader has known that these problems exist, and various efforts have been made to correct them. But the efforts of the NARC leaders and donor agencies have not succeeded, principally because the NARC continues to operate in a bureaucratic and political atmosphere that is not conducive to autonomous bodies – certainly not appropriate for an agricultural research institution. Autonomous bodies are intended to be free of political influence in the recruitment of personnel to their ranks and have greater flexibility both in the formulation of personnel and administrative policies as well as in their financial management. In fact, the very premise by which the NARC came into existence was the realization that effective agricultural research is not possible under the government bureaucracy of the Department of Agriculture under the MOA. Rarely has the NARC been given the flexibility that was intended, nor has it exercised that which it has. On the contrary, the recent amendment in by-laws has clearly revealed the narrow vision and utter lack of accountability or commitment to fairness towards all employees. The interests of the NARC seem to come second to the personal interests of some people whose only notable pursuit is to be attendant to political masters or just to hang around them for personal gain. The NARC cannot make a difference so long as it is under the grip of such political cronies.

The general feeling in the ministry is that an institution dependent on public funds should be under the control of the ministry. Although, this is not expressed publicly, it is a truism one can gather from the actions and behaviour of the ministry's bureaucrats. We talk of new social changes and the broadening of mental horizons but conservatism runs deep in the beliefs, behaviour and working style of the MOA bureaucrats.

Improved pay scales do provide incentives for scientific staff to produce quality research. But to our dismay, this is not the case in the NARC, since an effective evaluation and reward system is not in place. The situation is further complicated by "push and pull" from influential positions. This has essentially reduced the NARC to an institution that exists merely to carry out orders from above – an anti-thesis of the autonomous principles it is supposed to embody. The result is that good performance is never rewarded and poor performance is rarely punished. This is the most damaging weakness in the NARC. The consequences are disastrous. Leaders of the NARC lack the courage to stand up to political and bureaucratic intimidation thereby condemning the institution to mediocrity. It seems that the dream of our predecessors to make the NARC a centre of excellence shall remain a dream.

With such mediocrity and inefficiency in the NARC the full capacity of research scientists is rarely utilized. This state of affairs has had a serious demotivating and demoralizing impact on many young scientists. They are turned into idle assets with few, if any, career prospects in the NARC. The obvious consequence of this situation is brain drain, which threatens both the success and the sustainability of development activities.

In recent years, the NARC has turned into a political arena for ministers and secretaries to satisfy their egos and satiate their need for supremacy tearing the very fabric of institutional autonomy. To outsiders the NARS has lost its focus. These problems have been compounded by a lack of decisiveness on the part of the NARS leaders, who look for a "security blanket" in every decision to be made. Donors are confused by this state of affairs. Recently, representatives from an International Agricultural Research Centre (IARC) came to sign a memorandum of understanding but returned empty handed. No one among the management feels responsible for this shameful situation. What signal must NARS be sending to donors and international centres? Has the NARS management time to ponder? The latest evaluation mission of the World Bank project has reported the progress of the NARC component as unsatisfactory. This is a shrill warning that the NARC is in dire straits and needs a leader of strong conviction to rescue it from its pathetic situation.

Fortunately, all is not lost. There are very capable scientists within the NARS on whom government and donors have invested a fortune. The challenge is to put them to work in that field for which they are trained. At this juncture, steps to turn the wheels of progress for an autonomous NARC backward would be counter-productive to expectations, from agricultural research, envisioned in the APP, in the long run. Let us hope that the decisions of the new government in this regard will show some wisdom and vision. One likes to be surprised once in a while.

The Kathmandu Post – June 05, 1999

53

Poverty Alleviation and Agriculture

Every government that came in power, be it after the restoration of democracy or prior to it, has had claimed to its credit the significant economic and social achievements during its tenure in the government. In spite of such ostentatious claim the ground reality is that the numbers of the poor, landless and hungry people of the country are relentlessly increasing.

We all are aware that most of these unfortunate people live in rural areas where they are inevitably dependent on farming and related rural industries for their future hope of employment, higher income and better living standard. But unfortunately, many of them are now abandoning these hopes and migrating to cities, not in trickle but in torrent, where the limited urban services are not enough to cope with the exodus. This predicament has been further exacerbated by the existing political turmoil in the country.

There are countless historical and contemporary evidences to show that if a country like Nepal improves its agricultural productivity it at once increases job opportunities, both on-farm and off-farm that service farmers. Then, when the poor people find employment and gain a regular income, they spend much of their money on food steadily improving their health and general standard of living. Economic and social progress throughout the whole community, then, starts spinning off.

Since it is advances in agriculture that initially drive the engine of national economic development, the most pressing problem the country faces is how to improve the agricultural productivity. Looking at the agricultural advancement in developed countries one tends to think that plenty of fertilizers, irrigation water, and agricultural chemicals, combined with machines and high yielding varieties of crops would together do the trick.

However, experience has shown that the success of these so-called high energy input technologies of farming is often short-lived and, in the end, they lead to serious environmental degradation. Therefore, the challenge we all face today is learning how to produce higher yields of crops and livestock while still conserving essential natural resources, like soil, water, forests and bio-diversity, which will be needed for the survival of our future generations.

Although information on improved farming with sustainable technologies has increased in recent years, there are still many vital gaps in our knowledge, particularly in relation to some of the soils, indigenous crops and local pests and diseases found in the country. There is only one way of expanding knowledge of these essential matters and, therefore, of developing the higher yielding and sustainable farming technologies that are needed to generate jobs, incomes and exports. This knowledge can only come from the process of experimentation and trial-and-error, which constitute research.

As improved agricultural productivity provides the necessary basis of national economic progress, so does agricultural research provide the sustainable and profitable technologies that are the necessary bases of improved agricultural practices.

The economic and environmental returns from agricultural research are known to be greater than from other forms of public investment yet, in recent years, the government has reduced their funding for this activity, and this decline is continuing. This is true with bilateral and international agencies as well. The reason frequently given by aid donors is that the government does not accord a high priority to agricultural research in its own national expenditure or in the requests for development aid.

Therefore, there is no point in funding agricultural research in these countries when they are themselves unwilling to provide their own agricultural research systems with adequate resources. Does this not demand introspection of the psyche and attitude of the Ministry of Agriculture vis-à-vis agricultural research policy?

There is plenty of evidence to support the view that one of the most important long-term reasons why Nepalese agriculture performed so poorly has been the relative neglect of research and technology by the government. There is no doubt that ministers and political leaders have not sufficiently appreciated the importance of research in agriculture development.

When budget cuts in public expenditure have to be made, the government likes to cut first those items that do not cause antagonism and public fury. Clearly one such item is agricultural research. The budget cuts in agricultural research normally pass unnoticed, questions are not raised in parliament, the media remain silent, and there are no protest rallies and public demonstration on streets. Politicians always prefer to make decisions, which are easy and do not invite acrimonious criticism and protest. Therefore, one can only be baffled and frustrated by the seeming unwillingness of the government and politicians to respond in a rational manner to a serious issue that deserves attention.

Despite the fact that the funding needs of agricultural research are extremely modest in relation to most items of national expenditure, there is an inexplicable reluctance on the part of the government to fund this vital activity. For example, there is a widespread norm that countries should allocate at least 2% of their Agricultural Gross Domestic Product (AGDP) to agricultural research. Most developed countries spend over 2% of their AGDP on their own agricultural research, and they do this because the resultant improvements in farm efficiency make their farm produce more competitive in the market. However, in our case we are spending less than one half of 1% of AGDP on our national agricultural research systems.

The reality is that our farm productivity is being held back, our competitiveness in the market is being undermined, and our national prosperity is being unnecessarily limited because the agricultural research services are starved of the modest level of resources that they require. Recently, we have been discussing on the Poverty Alleviation Fund (PAF), a very much talked issue in the government's programme planning. Has the PAF duly taken note of the important role of agricultural research in poverty alleviation? Unless the decreasing trend in funding agricultural research remains unchanged, the battle on poverty will not be realized. The casualties of this situation will not be scientists but the poor people of the country. Therefore, support for agricultural research is not a matter of charity but it should be taken as wisdom and prudence.

The Kathmandu Post – January 22, 2004

54

Quo Vadis, NARC?

Agricultural research continues to receive low priority in the government's annual budget. Another ominous sign is that it is in danger of being pushed away from the development agenda of donors as well.

The decline in the importance of agricultural research appears in part due to the Nepal Agricultural Research Council (NARC) itself as it has failed to prove its worth by contributing to the national economy, since it has been incessantly indulging in the internal wrangling supported by partisan interest. It is also partly due to the conservatism that bestrides the Ministry of Agriculture (MoA) failing to recognize that the NARC can be a powerful engine in developing the agrarian economy like ours. The NARC always needed support of the MoA, but unfortunately from its very birth, lack of synergy and antagonism have remained as the unwritten decree of the MoA against the NARC.

In the research organization like the NARC, getting research work done calls for adequate fund and motivated scientists. But the partisan interest of the henchmen of the political parties has always made the NARC unstable by lobbying their masters to interfere in the appointment to the executive posts. This generic uncertainty has encouraged sycophancy, which is rampant in the NARC. This has taken its toll by masking the NARC's capability to contribute in the development of agriculture by enhancing the agricultural productivity. Beholding the pathetic plight of the NARC the scribe had once written in this column (*The Kathmandu Post*, June, 1999), "...NARC cannot make a difference so long as it is under the grip of such political cronies."

Because of this, the capacity of research scientists in the NARC is rarely fully utilized. This has rendered the NARC as an unproductive and inefficient institution. The same scientists, when given an opportunity to work in international research centres, have had excelled. What makes them so productive there, when many of them are less effective at home? This underlines the critical need of improving the NARC's structural and research management paradigm.

It is now an open secret that whenever the government changes, the minions of political parties start stooping at the doorstep of their masters asking them to purge CEO and place their acquiescent to such positions. This practice is so pervasive that one finds research hijacked by politics. The zenith of politicization was attainded during the minority government of the UML. Till the date, this has remained as a festering sore in the NARC that has relegated a supposed-to-be centre of excellence to mediocrity.

Today, the NARC is in a complete mess. There is hardly any leader visible, who is tall enough with independent stature, to steer the NARC out of this quagmire. The present senior generation in the NARC aspiring for leadership has failed to show their visionary leadership to look beyond themselves and their petty interests. They are all interested to sit at the captain's chair for a few more years knowing that this Titanic is sinking. They are not remorseful for their inefficiency to avoid the disaster. A feeling of general hopelessness pervades that no one can save the NARC from its fated perdition.

The NARC is in the process of selecting a new executive director (ED) now. Whether he will be from within or outside the NARC system is a matter of anybody's guess. At present, the NARC is rife with rumors that the MoA is intriguing with the selection body for a candidate possibly from out of the NARC system. The feeling is in the air. You can almost reach out and touch it when one talks about it in the ministry. An invisible, yet palpable, apple-card is obvious on the drawing board of the ministry, NARC observers suspect. A scientist from the NARC, an aspirant for the position, under the condition of anonymity expresses his frustration about the motive of the MoA and says that they will sideline them even following the NARC's by-laws as there is no one there to stand against it.

No one in the NARC believes that the selection body is capable of functioning independently and can select a candidate without being biased. The members of the body are the products of the Panchyat era of autocratic functioning and their working style is surreptitious and not transparent. They are all-time servers and their motive is not the wellbeing of the NARC but their master's satisfaction.

It was a calculated move on the part of the MoA also to fill the position of the ED without consulting the NARC when there is an absence of whistle-blowers. On the part of the MoA, this is its another activism in the guise of a do-gooder to put the NARC under its thumb.

Because of this damning politicization, the NARC has lost its credibility and focus. It has failed to transform itself according to the time. As national and political boundaries are becoming blurred with the globalization, the NARC should have effectively modified itself to reflect such changes for its growth and development. This calls for a bold and visionary leadership that the NARC requires at present.

The NARC has been squandering time in internal politicking and it is clear now that the cronies of political parties are office bearers in this organization. Hence, the credibility of the NARC is not going to be restored unless the concerned officials criticize themselves for the harm they had done to it and stop maneuvering it for their personal and political gains. It is certain that the NARC is not going to get a second chance to justify itself. If the credibility is not restored soon, the NARC will be stuck in a cul-de-sac. Let wisdom prevail.

The Kathmandu Post – August 16, 2005

55

Reform and Perform or Perish

The sense of *déjà vu* is ineluctably palpable in the Nepal Agricultural Research Council (NARC), after the result of the constituent assembly poll, as soon as one happens to meet the officials of the management team. The Maoist's accession to power is yet another premonition to the officials, when the allegiances of the mandarins to the likely incoming government are kicking their heels in anticipation that the next NARC's leader is their go-getter.

Ever since its genesis the NARC, unequivocally a scientific institution, has been mired with incumbent and opposition politics. Because of the pervasive situation in the NARC, its integrity as an apex body is at nadir. Much to one's chagrin, the dramatis personae in the vaudeville of the NARC's salvation politics are mostly non-researchers who have hijacked its image of being a research organization. Of course, a few smug researchers also do play this game, but a large chunk of its scientists, who truly believes in professionalism and is indifferent to politicization of the institution, remains uncomfortably perched on a fence.

Although the Ministry of Agriculture (MoA) tries to display an avuncular face in regard to the NARC, the stark reality is that there is hardly any synergy between them. This is a very unfortunate situation where agricultural research is an important part of overall agenda of agriculture development of the government which the MoA is responsible for. When the NARC functions inefficiently — be it due to resource crunch or politicization or internal wrangling, one may not observe brouhaha on the MoA's face but the snigger is clearly visible that unravels the untold agenda.

Politics in the NARC is ubiquitous and so is taking its toll by rendering it redundant in national scenario when enhancement of agricultural productivity is taken into consideration. The government has substantially reduced its funding in real terms, making agricultural research increasingly dependent on external support. As foreign support is ephemeral, the NARC is left forlorn and its credibility is dwindling. Never before has it suffered for shortage of fund for non-salary costs, as it has today due to lack of a dependable funding. The frustrating effect of this predicament is that the NARC has been reduced to a research bureaucracy, where research scientists sit idle in their offices because there is no fund to travel to the field or to buy supplies for their experiments and laboratories.

The working conditions and incentives are not only poor but also inadequate at all levels. More importantly promotions are not linked to performance. Even when performance is evaluated and rewarded the NARC is restricted to follow the beaten path of bureaucratic criteria without much regard to the relevance of academic publications and the researches for developing products that respond to clients' needs. This has discouraged good researchers and superior research managers with obvious result ensuing brain drain that is shrinking the NARC's pool of well-trained and dedicated scientists. Very soon the NARC is going to be fraught with void of experienced and devoted scientists. This situation has relegated it to a club of dead woods interested in politicking rather than doing research. Not very long, when the NARC's staffs went for sit-in, leaders of political parties visited and cajoled them as if they were the members of their party; what does that indicate? Time has come that stoic and dedicated staffs of the NARC should do their soul-searching. Should the NARC be managed by professional research managers or under the influence of trade union like staff unions which are all the time gyrating around the leaders of political parties?

The NARC is arguably one of the most important institutional developments in the history of agricultural research. Even with its many faults, it is the best investment that the government and the donors have done in agricultural sector. It has a potential of making things different when it gets a working environment. Why then are the government and donors losing interest and leaving it forlorn? In spite of the NARC's contributions in enhancing agricultural productivity which are praiseworthy and well documented, a number of things have also gone very wrong. The most damaging development has been its incessant politicization and loss of focus.

The NARC's priorities are not focused and it has thinly spread its resources on many commodities and research issues. Evidences strongly suggest that this is not a cost-effective approach, particularly when the NARC talks about adaptive research. The NARC should remain on guard to prove itself an intelligent borrower of technologies developed in neighboring countries and elsewhere. But much of what the NARC does in technology development, as opposed to technology transfer, amounts to wasteful duplication. This, however, does not mean that the NARC should refrain from technology development; rather the question is the extent it should involve in it. Hard choices on what to beef up and what to lay-off are needed.

Although the NARC in its vision plan talks about commercialization of agriculture, it has failed to respond to the demands of commercial farming and export opportunities. Increasingly, the challenge is not only to enhance productivity in agriculture alone, but in the entire chain from farming through marketing. This demands a reorientation in the NARC's approach. Looking at the present situation of the NARC, where staff unions like frontline outfits of political parties dominate the show, it seems very unlikely that the NARC will be able to respond to these new challenges.

The NARC has been given some working autonomy, but still conforms to a bureaucratic way of doing its business. Decision-making is overly centralized. What it needs for its effective performance is business-like governance where research managers are given much flexibility with strict accountability for delivering results. But for many reasons, demand-driven governance has remained an elusive approach for the NARC.

In order to make agricultural research more effective the NARC must transform itself to be more relevant to client needs. This calls for institutional reform for which champions, dedicated visionaries and persistent change agents are required who can build the needed coalitions to push it ahead. Surrounded by dwarfs only, an organization cannot become a giant.

As the NARC is a government agency it can enjoin reform or obliterate it. Most of the Council members appointed by ministers are more like cornucopia rather than on their merit. Because of this situation, the NARC has not been able to benefit from the devolution of power, though inadequate, that the government has made. In order to effectively avail this opportunity the Council should be represented more by clients and professionals rather than ex-officio of the government entities, as the case is now.

With cosmetic changes only it is very likely that the NARC, we know it now, would cease to exist as an apex body in future. Bold transformations from institutional to statutory reform and attitude in the ministry will be required to enable it to effectively carry out its mission and to merit the financial and political support the NARC so badly needs.

The Kathmandu Post – May 20, 2008

56

Agriculture in the Doldrums

During last fiscal year when the Ministry of Agriculture and Development (MoAD) had announced the record harvest of foodgrain crops, officials in the MoAD were brimming over about getting the second wind. But the euphoria proved an evanescent phenomenon this fiscal year when the Central Bureau of Statistics (CBS) unveiled the National Account Estimate projecting the economic growth trailing at 3.56 percent, a dip to six-year low when it was 2.75 percent, according to the preliminary estimation. The projected growth rate is far below what the government had initially targeted. Delayed budget and poor performance of agriculture coupled with slow down in industrial growth were the *raison d'être* the CBS has identified for this downfall. The estimate projected that agriculture will grow by a mere 1.26 percent against 4.94 percent growth rate of last year. The non-agriculture sector has performed slightly better (4.98 percent) this year as compared to last year (4.15 percent).

On the surface, the CBS projection is a routine analysis depicting the inconsistency, a usual phenomenon that is ingrained with our economic growth rate. But when it is viewed from the population growth rate vis-à-vis the growing number of food deficit districts, the flickering statistics of 1.26 percent agricultural growth flashes the going will get tough in the coming days. The writing on the wall is loud and clear that the per capita availability of food, even now which does not commensurate with the value of 420 kg per year recommended by Agriculture Perspective Plan (APP), will further trail behind making the problem of food and nutrition in the country more ominous. This situation is growing over time and the hills and mountains are the regions that bear the brunt of food deficit most every year, where the annual food production is not adequate for the consumption for even six months. The rhetoric of the MoAD officials saying the presence of enough food stock is not going to fill the empty stomach of people in the hills and mountains unless it is transported to these regions which is a Herculean task for the government due to skewed distribution system owing to the rugged terrain and rudimentary infrastructure. While situation under food supply front is depressing the recent decision of the government to deregulate wheat export is not only uncalled for, it is an affront to the basic rights of people in general, and hills and mountains in particular, to get food. The government is insensitive in making decision as who should be the primary beneficiary of our agricultural production – foreign or domestic consumers? The government seems to be suffering from withdrawal symptom when there was enough food in the country and we were exporting it till early eighties.

Despite more than five decades of our planned development agriculture is turning out to be one of the most neglected professions against our old saying Uttam kheti, Madhyam byopar... (Farming is the best occupation, second best is business and working for someone else is the worst). Since farming is increasingly becoming an unviable profession and farmers across the country are getting a beating for adopting this occupation, young generation from the Terai or the hills and mountain alike are least interested to take up this profession. Instead they are ready to toil at the desert of Gulf Countries or hostile environment of other countries as migrant workers. Because of such situation, land is left untilled due to shortage of working hands. Women and old generation are left in the village to do the farming activities to the best of their physical capacity. The situation is deteriorating year after year, thus the entire farming sector is heading for a collapse, if no long-term remedial measures are taken up by the government.

The MoAD, running through ad hocism seems to be overwhelmed by policy fatigue, has no plan to address soil fatigue as has been developed by overexploitation of nutrients and organic matter in intensive cropping areas. The Chure bhabar range is turning into barren land with the threat of desertification looming large due to wanton tree felling, overwhelming soil and nutrient wash, receding water table and unmanageable operation of stone quarries. The President Ram Baran Yadav's unremitting zeal to reclaim the Chure region had heralded a glad tiding but Nepalese bureaucrats have turned it into a hasty afterthought.

The sluggish performance of agriculture sector is an indication in itself a lackluster performance of various leading public institutions viz., the Ministry of Agriculture and Development (MoAD), the Nepal Agricultural Research Council (NARC), the Department of Agriculture (DoA), the Department of Irrigation (DoI), the Institute of Agriculture and Animal Sciences (IAAS) and various input supplying institutions, unable to discharge their responsibility to effect the desired output. These lead institutions with their mandate to boost agriculture development are so inefficient and marred with inherent problem of politicization that major restructuring and change in the work culture is needed before these agencies perform as a functional catalyst. They are seen more active and attentive in protecting their own turf than being responsive to the farmers' demand. Some how the quintessential elements for enhancing foodgrain production namely technology generation, verification and delivery to farmers; availability of right inputs at right time and adequate quantities and training component (on the job and academic) do not seem to be in sync.

The NARC is responsible for generating new technologies that increase farmers' production and productivity. Much to the farmers' chagrin there has been no technological breakthrough that can augment the yield of major foodgrains as it happened in many countries during the green revolution stint. Our farmers had to satisfy only with the trickle down effect of the green revolution, let alone its practice, in spite of the collaboration with several International Research Institutions. The NARC should have played a key role in reviving the Nepalese agriculture; instead it has turned into a symbol of technology fatigue due to too much bureaucratization and political high-handedness – a pastime sport of our political leaders.

To boost agricultural production, one of the major factors is availability of land, a finite natural resource, which is getting scarce year by year turning farming a struggle for existence for farmers. The government of chief justice-turned-chairman of the council of ministers should have shown sensitivity to threatening food shortage and moved with unusual alacrity to stem the rot. Such policy initiatives are not visible in the recent budget address of the bureaucrat-turned-finance minister. Experts are not impressed with his budget speech as there are too little new measures the government has envisioned to address the looming food shortage in the country. Thus by default commodity prices will spiral up making lives of common people further miserable.

The problem of such nature and magnitude can not be addressed by a mindset of business as usual and fill up the blank attitude. In order to respond to such crisis one needs to have an out-of-the-box thinking which was clearly not visible in the recent address of the finance minister as well as in the working style of the technocrat-turned-bureaucrat government. Thus more and more marginal farmers will be forced to opt out their current farming profession and the young generation, which has no attraction towards farming, will be tempted to go out of the country in torrents as migrant workers. Who should be responsible to contain them and provide a dignified environment to work in the country?

Telegraphnepal.com – June 4, 2013

57

Postscript

"Let us pray that prudence prevails upon them (CA members) this time."

These were the words said by the common people of the street when they watched the coverage of the proceedings inside the CA.

"Otherwise the nation is done for!"

The statement echoed the fears of the most Nepalis who witnessed the gruesome act inside the House on the night of 19 and 22 January, 2015. In the wake of political dalliance of the Maoists and its alliance the concomitant circumstances justify that the above words are proving to be prophetic.

Nepal is struggling with embittered political transition to transform itself from an exclusionary and centralized state to a more inclusive and federal one. This post conflict transition, a precursor to state transformation, has not been linear and thus it is floundering through achievements and setbacks. Concatenations suggest that it is unlikely to be completed in short period of time, in spite of the political leaders' commitments which sounds platitudinal. As the internecine transition remains protracted, the country is in a fix with the interim arrangement which was not envisaged for long haul.

When the leaders of political parties practiced consensual politics sincerely, unprecedented achievements have been registered in the Nepali politics. As the NC and the then CPN (ML) launched the first peoples' movement together in 1989, it forced King Birendra to agree to remain as a constitutional monarch, although, in practical term the state power was never handed over by the king to the institution of peoples' representative in toto. There comes the constitution of 1990 which was written in consensus with the political parties. The military, the source of state power, remained under the king. The Maoists, as it did not accept the then constitution, when could not assert themselves in democratic polity, they started their revolution in defiance of the then constitution with an objective to establish a state of dictatorship of proletariats. Wasting more than 14,000 Nepali lives they realized that it is difficult to achieve their goal due to several internal and external factors and thus they went for a paradigm shift that gave them a safe landing.

They entered the mainstream politics through a consensual deal with seven party alliance, known as a historical 12-points agreement. Together with the democratic forces they fought against the usurpation of power by King Gyanendra. This consensual approach proved instrumental in taking the second peoples' revolution to its zenith and forced the accidental King Gyanendra to abdicate his power in favour of people by restoring the parliament again. In the light of the political transformation that took place in the country suggests that when the democratic and progressive forces work together rising above the partisan line epoch-making changes are possible. These forces, oblivious to this fact, when wrangling with one another are encouraging ultra radicals of the both sides to raise their voices. This is definitely not a good omen to the democratic transformation the country is looking for.

The political synergy that had obliged the king to succumb to public opinion must continue if the constitution that the people are aspiring for, at all, to be written by the CA II. But the recent developments that happened inside and outside the CA do not send an encouraging message to people at large indicating lack of trust among the leaders, who once were co-traveler in bringing the tectonic change in the country. Consensus does not function in a trust deficit environment. The Maoists, although, pay lip service to democracy often give rise to widespread distrust as their leaders continue to subscribe their dogmatic ideology in the wake of their agenda when not accepted in the House by the majority. This is rather a consensual flirtation that does not help to create ambience for trust.

The story of the Madhesi leaders, who are one of the game changers in bringing republic in the country, could not rise above petty partisan interests and failed to advance beyond the agenda of ethnic federalism, has led to polarization among different ethnic communities and marginal groups that inhabit the Terai since generations. As far as the *janjati* in the hills are concerned they are no different than their Madhesi counterpart. While advocating such festering politics of polarization by leaders of various hues, balkanization is fraught with danger for posterity. Bogged by their ego and partisan interests, leaders of the political parties failed to show foresight in the larger interests of the nation and people. Common people are of opinion that this is a subversion of their mandate by the political leaders.

If one sincerely believes in democracy, there is always a way out for settling differences through absolute consensus, if not maximum consensus or if one foresees that consensus can not address all issues to their satisfaction, keeping aside the agreed agenda, the debatable issues could be put for majority voting, a quintessential device to settle conflicts by reason, argument and persuasion. After all, the constitution assembly itself is a result of popular consent through ballot-box. Therefore, the political leaders of the CA II must read the writings on the wall and deliver the constitution that they have committed or else be prepared to be damned by the common people.

The Great Earthquake, that hit Nepal over the weekend of April 25-26, 2015 has been like a scene from hell. Villages and towns, temples and buildings – small and high-rises have turned into rubble. Mountains, that stood majestic consuming the surroundings, are washed away by the earthquake triggered landslides, are replaced by starring lifeless void. More than 8500 people have lost their lives, 16000 injured and more than three hundred thousand houses have been destroyed with more than two million people displaced. The river banks of Pashupatinath Temple and other parts of the country are lit up with funeral pyres reminding us life is in immortal agony. From seismic point of view this earthquake (7.9 Richter scale) was a thousand times more powerful than the Hiroshima of 6.32 magnitudes.

Faultlines in Nepali Politics

The overdue earthquake, expert had been foretelling, finally hit Nepal on April 25, 26 and May 12, 2015 with several after-shocks that have exceeding 4000 number still continue to thud and thump everyday making people to hold their breath. My eight- and nine-year-old grand daughters and two-year-old grandson still sleep with their go-bags ready besides their beds. Though the earthquake was expected, nevertheless, it was not easy to predict its time and place which is very much like our treacherous political leaders who are so infamous for their unpredictability in making a voltface. It was a very big and monoster quake as we call it Maha (Great) Earthquake and nothing can prepare a nation for a devastation of such magnitude. It has not only wrecked natural fury rather opened up political, diplomaic, and economical faultlines in Nepali Politics. According to the World Bank 700,000 to 982,000 people of quake affected area are likely to slip back into the poverty trap due to loss of their assets and income generating opportunities pushing the poverty rate from 25 to somewhere 28 percent.

To match the unprecedented devastation, extraordinary relief efforts have been initiated. Helps have been pouring in from various levels – individual, institutional and state. Our neighbour and friendly countries sent help generously first and left the details to be worked later so that as many as possible lives could be saved – a true humanitarian gesture one can call it when a friend is in real need. The government tried its best, may be not perfect, to regulate the relief operation as well as institutions and individuals – national and international. Everyone wanted to help and associate in the relief operation to show their compassion in assuaging the sufferings and pain of millions of hapless earthquake victims. Crack teams of more than 4000 persons from 34 countries comprising of rescue, military and medical personnels arrived in Kathmandu with their necessary equipments on a very short notice request of the government. Within six hours of disaster, India was first to arrive here with its crack team and relief materials. The Indian team has done marvelous job of rescue and relief which Nepali will always remember as a true neighbourly gesture when a friend is in real need. But the paradox is the media that came along with the team due to lack of finesse and its avuncular demeanour in dealing with the situation brought indignation not only in the Nepali social media but in India also as famous writer and critic like Shoba De and historian Ramchandra Guha critically wrote about it. One should not be oblivious of the facts, as there is an anti-Pakistani element engrained in Indian psyche, so is anti- Indian element has been implanted in Nepali psyche by the undemocratic rulers of the past in the pretext of national unit and sovereignty. This jingo element is always in look-out for such opportunity where they can fan India bashing disregarding the fact that whenever the going gets tough, it is India who has always extended helped to Nepal. No one can obliterate this fact.

The commendable job of relief and rescue operation that India had carried out is by no way can be underestimated. Nepalis are appreciative of Indian promptness and generosity, no doubt, but often feel resented sense of dependency. Despite its strong cultural engagement the relationship with India is of love and hate which Nepal always fraught with. The natural disaster had provided India an opportunity to cultivate a confidence in Nepali psyche through Prime Minister Modi's neighbour first approach, but unfortunately due to media's over-reach and crack team's uncalled for approach were not taken by Nepalis positively. Many Indian friends asked me why there is an anti-India sentiment here in spite of our sincere effort to help Nepal. I simply laughed and told them that you present yourself as a big brother, whereas we like to see you as an elder brother.

We know that India is worried with the growing influence of China in Nepal but so is China with India's putting finger in every Nepali pie. China, traditionally concerned with the only Tibetan refugees in Nepal, has started to show its interest visibly in Nepali politics. China complained to Nepal about the Indian helicopter engaged in relief operation entered their sky. With this they also sent their relief and rescue team through air and land routes followed by American team. This is the first time that foreign militaries have landed in Nepal on the request of the government for humanitarian work. It is an open secret that for all three countries Nepal is strategically important and therefore they helped with open heart. On the other hand international organizations, NGOs and NRN are putting pressure on to the government to carry out the relief operation on their own blaming the government as inept and corrupt. But government has decided a one door policy in the relief operation which is not only rational but a question linked with the country's dignity and sovereignty as well.

The relief and rescue works carried out by the friendly countries deserve profound appreciation. The government was in the forefront of all of these operations. With such unprecedented scale of relief operation, it is not uncommon to hear some divergent narratives and negative anecdotes about the government's response to handling of disaster mitigation. Such narratives and whisper reflect some of the faultlines in Nepali politics. The complex politics surrounding the response to enormous rehabilitation and reconstruction efforts met will determine if the massive relief operation will bring the country together or return Nepal to the politics of partisanship and festering polarization. One should not be surprised if the earthquake provides a new outlook to what federalism and state restructuring will entail.

In the aftermath of the Great Earthquake Machiavellian expediency of political leaders has also come into forefront manifesting their dissembler character. The opposition party led by the UCPN(M) has started hobnobbing with the CPN-UML, an alliance in the present government, advocating the imperative of a "national unit government" censuring the present government for its ineffectiveness in handling the earthquake tragedy. On the other hand, Dr. Baburam Bhattarai, number two, in UCPN(M) is floating the idea of formation of a Disaster Management Authority to oversee the relief and reconstruction activities.

People have become much conscious now that they understand the meaning in between the line of these leaders' desultory arguments. Since people have been watching them flirting with the word consensus for the last eight years for their political aggrandizement. Therefore, they are not convinced with the change of the government at this hour of national crisis without forging a broad consensus on the constitution making.

As Nepal has been struggling with the long drawn provisionality due to the absence of constitution and the ennui has been the consuming tragedy of the Constitution Assembly. Under such circumstances, the Great Earthquake has become the catalyst in generating an unprecedented sense of collective responsibility among the ruling and the opposition parties. Perhaps the earthquake, a nature's fury, has provided the expedient leaders a message: people are more important than politics. This has helped to break the thaw among the four political forces (NC, NCP-UML, UCPN-M, and MJF-D). They have arrived to an understanding to fast-track the constitution making process. The common people are watching the development cautiously as they have been hearing such rhetoric since the day of the first CA in the past. These belligerent leaders, in one or another pretext, failed to produce the constitution they had promised to people. Therefore, common people were not in mood to accept them on their face value.

But this time it seems that prudence has prevailed upon them and they have surprised the critics of Nepali politics. The fast-tract functioning of the four political forces has yielded much awaited upshot. Much to the surprise of everyone, a 16-point agreement has been reached among these forces which would now clear the path of constitution making. The political parties which were pole apart in their stand on federalism, form of governance and other nitty-gritty from day one of the CA flew off at a tangent is a matter to delve for the political analysts for posterity.

Since dissent is a common phenomenon in democracy, the fast-track constitution making was also not free from censure. The Madhesi and *janjati* parties, the alliance in opposition parties led by UCPN-M, had resented it and submitted a memorandum to the President stating that it has violated the spirit and provisions of the Interim constitution and asked him to intervene as the guardian of the constitution. But looking at the rut the politics had been for the past eight years, a sense of hoplessness pervaded across the nation about getting the constitution. People are of opinion that if the constitution was not delivered this time, it would be rather difficult to get it for a long time in the future. People were hauling leaders over coal for their ineptness and thus they were waiting for the D-day keeping their finger cross.

The Madhesi Beachhead

Aware of the people's mood, the coalition government of Sushil Koirala did not dare to flirt this time in the pretext of consensual politics. And there came the first constitution of the Republic ever drafted by people's representatives. No doubt, promulgation of the constitution was a first step forward but it had a devious path ahead. The taste of the pudding one can judge only after he eats it. Albeit, the Madhesi Morcha refused to accept the constitution and boycotted the final voting on it, the Constitution Assembly (CA) adopted the tabled draft with amendments agreed upon by the House with a thumping majority of almost ninety percent. It was a history in itself.

The Madhesi Morcha and its allies conjoined by Tharu went on the street burning the constitution to demonstrate their resentment followed by various violent agitations of *band* and *dharna*. Concatenations suggest that neither side is willing to relent. It pushed the opposition to harden its position following more aggressive means. We watch almost every day in our television tragic news of arson, brick-batting, baton charge and occasional loss of life. The coercive agitation has passed nearly six months and turned slowly to humanitarian problem on one hand while pushing the country to slow-bleeding on the other hand.

The quintessential of democracy that encourages majority rule accompanied by respect for the rights of minorities has been blighted by the ugly and violent agitations that continue hitherto in the pretext of their demands being not addressed in the constitution. No doubt, some of their demands are genuine and justified. But when more than fourty- five precious lives including that of security personal are wasted, one is obliged to question – do such gory agitations merit enough for the cause they have been advocating? Protest and demonstration for one's rights is totally rational but intimidating others fundamental rights is not accepted in democracy. Thus, are these events mere coincidental or else collusion?

Being a sovereign nation, the constitution drafting is a prerogative of Nepal and its people. More so, when it had been drafted, it was an open exercise where no skeletons hidden in the cup-board. Once the constitution was announced, the Madhesi Morcha and its allies staged a sit-in at the no-man's land of Nepal-India border. Earlier, had there been any kind of hindrance or traffic log-jam on the border, police of both the sides with joint coordinated action helped each other to clear the disturbance. But this time Indian police not only refused to cooperate but allowed the protestors to receive their daily meals - a BJP local activist opened a *langar* in his premise - and shelter and turned a blind eye when they threw stones and petrol bombs on Nepal police from Indian soil holding all norms of international relation at bay. This has rendered human and vehicular movement impossible from either side. Every time when Nepal lodged a complaint, India smugly brushed off saying there is no problem in our side it is the security problem at Nepal side that is holding the traffic flow. Seemingly it was so, but the reason underside is not what one beholds on the ground. Therefore, the major casualty of the apathetic Indian complacence to Nepal's distress is truth, as whole world is aware of the verity.

India should not forget the history that its own constitution was not adopted with such overwhelming majority as has been the case of Nepal. It is always desirable to write a constitution in full consensus, but when it is not possible due to diverse of opinion maximum consensus is the democratic way out. When the draft was ready to table in the CA, India's action to rush its Foreign Secretary to Kathmandu was viewed by intelligentsia in both the countries as peremptory stand of India taking Nepal as its backyard. In spite of, Nepal's patient hearing to Prime Minister Modi's envoy, Nepal had its obligation towards its people and thus went ahead with the draft constitution in the CA. With the amendments the CA adopted it by more than two-third majority. Whole world congratulated Nepal, but India sulkily noted it showing its dissatisfaction which was writ large. This was the turning point in the present protracted crisis where India's insinuation helped the Madhesi agitation to be intransigent.

Who is right and who is wrong, history will decide in the posterity. But for a dispassionate observer like me, on one hand, it is an utter failure of Nepali's diplomacy to take India into confidence and convince them to what extent the constitution is accommodative to Madhesi demands, on the other hand, one finds lack of finesse and subtlety in handling Modi's neighbourhood policy following the beaten path of the Congress(I) era. In the entire fiasco China - a mute spectator - without speaking a single word reaped the advantage of anti-India rhetoric that extremists have been flogging constantly in the name of Indian blockade. The common people who are bearing the brunt of border logjam in terms of physical hardship and humanitarian problems may not sustain for long time and slowly fall into the trap of extremists design. If it happens, India will lose Nepal even to a greater extent than it had during the monarchial era.

The media in both the countries are busy in protecting their own turf and failed to create public opinion based on the whole truth. Much to the dismay of common people here, Prime Minister Modi's words contrast sharply with his action in the case of Nepal-India relation which he had so eloquently articulated in the Constituent Assembly. Critics here are of opinion that India's tacit support to Madhesi agitation has not only antagonized Nepali psyche but also deepened the Pahad-Madhes divide further. What has gone wrong to Modi's *Rishi man* (saintly attitude) who had gained him laurels when he said, in our Constituent Assembly, how India can remain happy when its neighbour Nepal is in trouble? Was it a *jumla* only or a sincere statement to break the chilling estrangement of last seventeen years between two trusted neighbours? Be it Pahad or Madhes whole country was rapt in his stump oratory. It was like *veni, vidi, vici* for Modi. Why a country so warm and affable to Prime Minister Modi six months ago suddenly went to hash-tag: Back off India. Something terrible must have happened and to find it out India needs to introspect the handling of the entire episode by its plenipotentiaries.

So far the Madhesi Morcha, spearing the present agitation, is concerned; it is difficult to define it in any precise form. It is, and has been, an amalgam of political parties and view-points leading to a mix of Marxist, socialist, liberal democrats, and even anarchists. Thus the Morcha has more 'revolutionary' than 'constitutional' who do not buzz from their hard line and trying to establish a beachhead within Madhes keeping an eye on the Madhesi block-vote. They do talk about negotiation but they are intransigent for any compromise on their stand – a practice universal to make any negotiation success. Due to such ambivalent perception of Madhesi leaders the agitation is slowly slipping away towards anarchists. Looking at the nature of the present agitation one could feel that a totalitarian idea that there is no such thing as law, there is only power, is taking root among the Madhesi agitators. Lawlessness is in the increase and political lawlessness particularly so. The agitators want to make their case not by ballot-box and persuasion but increasingly by resort to direct action. Of course the Madhesi leaders talk about crisis, but the word crisis has lost its urgent meaning to them. The solution of the present crisis lies on a simple message when Madhesi leaders get it: the people are more important than politics.

Not Yet Clicking

The Madhes agitation that started with a clarion call for establishing Madhesi identity, rights and inclusiveness has ushered in black marketing of essential goods on an unprecedented scale. To get their demands fulfilled, the leaders did not hesitate to strangulate the population at large by choking the border points, India's implicit support, a strategy avoided even during war, leading to a psychological chasm between the Hill and Madhes population. In future the Madhesi leaders may join with the establishment to share power, as there is no permanent friend or foe in politics, but the deep scar left between the two communities will not be healed some time soon.

The first federal constitution, promulgated by the second Constitution Assembly on September 20, 2015, as an immediate consequence of the Madhes agitation, was amended by the Constitution Assembly turned Parliament in three months. The amendment tried to address two out of the three important concerns the Madhesi Front raised: assigning electoral constituencies in relation to population and inclusive representation. The third issue–delineation of the boundaries of the two states carved in Madhes–was conceded to be resolved in three months time through a high level political instrument set up by political parties in consensus.

When the amendment was passed, optimism was rife that stability would be restored. But the Madhesi Front which has turned the country in a state of stasis by blocking the border repudiated the amendment, claiming it did not address their demands, a claim that found very few takers even in the Madhes itself. The recent visit of these leaders to Bihar is a clear manifestation of their despondency. When the agitation was petering out, reports were pouring in that the agitation is slipping away from the control of Madhesi leaders and this has been confirmed by the recent events of attack on the houses of the NC leaders in Janakpur and elsewhere in the country. Many more C. K. Rauts may be waiting in the wings to catch on deep-rooted ethnic allegiance steeped in prejudice and social backwardness. A situation has been created where it is like riding a tiger, not knowing how to get off without being eaten.

The Madhes movement of 2006 did establish the republican agenda. But to the dismay of every one, in the second Constitution Assembly election these leaders were rejected in their own bastion – Madhes – by the Madhesi voters as they failed to rise above I-me-myself brand of politics and showing off their individual egos larger than their size. Since then, not knowing how they will fare in the next parliamentary election, they are in a fix and may use all gimmicks to regain the ground lost in the Madhes. They know another loss of vote could wipe them out altogether posing an existential problem for them. This may explain why the agitation that started with big bang when ended unceremoniously, Madhesi *vox populi* did not make any resentment rather they acquiesced in. The mood is up beat in the Madesh as the repertoire of the agitation is slowing down. Nevertheless, the hard core Madhesi leaders haunted by the withdrawal system are trying to rewrite the script of another agitation bracing themselves up to realign in a grand alliance. This narrative one finds in to-day's Madhes, as the Front wants to retain the pressure on the establishment to gain from the momentum impelled by the blockade. But no one can tell how long the kettle can be kept boiling when the *vox populi* in Madhes is against another blockade. Otherwise the life there is turning from as usual to normal now.

As for India, a friend in need, always associated with political transition here when tried to play a role of devil's advocate got entangled in the political mess not by default but by political design. India, showing its interest in Nepal's constitution making process, under a veil, started acting as an external equalizer but ended up being an external destabilizer. This situation provided the anti-India element here an opportunity to trout out their theory that India's sleuth agencies like RAW and hawks of the South block are the true masterminds of the blockade and the genuine architects of the one Madhes one Pradesh who have been instilling this divisive idea into Madhesi leaders. But nearly six months long agitation with border blockade ended up little better than a damp squib as Nepal's mainstream political parties were hardly prepared for the gerrymandering on their agenda that has seed of secession inside dormant at present.

Since the blockade has been lifted now, I tried to find who benefited from the blockade of a landlocked nation yet resurrecting from a devastating earthquake. The answer was invariably, if anyone it is black marketers.

People here are pained physically and traumatized emotionally due to the blockade. Reconstruction and development activities of the government have been pushed back and the country's economy may take decade to recover. Inflation hit double-digits loosing millions of job. The number of poor will increase in millions crossing the poverty line. Nepal did not gain anything out of the siege. India, the impresario of the melodrama also failed to gain anything either politically or strengthening relation between the two countries. In the opinion of former ambassador to India Dr. Bhekh Bahadur Thapa – if Nepal suffered in terms of economy, India suffered damage in terms of goodwill. India seems to have realized it went too far and thus India's External Affairs Minister Shushma Swaraj held a meeting with the Prime Minister of Nepal K.P. Sharma Oli, as a damage control effort, when she was in Kathmandu to pay last homage to our late Prime Minister Sushil Koirala. Perhaps the biggest loser in this dramatic episode was the Madhesi Front, the so called organizer of the border blockade. It had consistently refuted and flaunted that blockade has nothing to do with India. It is their home-grown stratagem. But when India lifted the last blockade point at Birgunj–Raxaul Friendship Bridge, the Front found it aghast and tried to resume it. As Indian authority did not support them and drove them off from the bridge, they had to relent meekly announcing officially the suspension of the agitation after two days.

During his visit to India in February 2016, Prime Minister of Nepal K.P. Sharma Oli tried to clear the misunderstanding between the two countries while having a dialogue with Indian Prime Minister Narendra Modi in New Delhi. Oli is learnt to have assured that the pending issues would be addressed in a time-bound manner. The conversation took place weeks after Nepal's parliament passed two constitutional amendments which are expected to address the grievances of the Madhesis and other minorities. On combating terrorism, the two sides agreed to fight growing extremism and terrorism.

Index